IN THE GLORY OF HIS PRESENCE

*Walking in the Radiance of
God's Presence From Glory to Glory*

PETER LENGWE

ISBN:
Softcover: 978-1-972299-57-9
Hardback: 978-1-972299-58-6
eBook: 978-1-972299-56-2

For permission requests, visit and write to the publisher at:

Peter Lengwe | THE BREAD OF LIFE GLOBAL MINISTRIES

ACKNOWLEDGMENTS

To the God of Glory,

the One who dwells in unapproachable light,

yet in unfathomable mercy draws near to those who seek Him—

I give You all honor, all praise, and all the glory.

Every revelation in this book,

every sentence birthed in prayer,

every chapter breathed out of Your presence,

belongs to You alone.

Without Your Spirit, nothing could be written;

without Your grace, nothing could be understood.

To Jesus Christ,

the King of Glory and the Lamb upon the throne,

thank You for opening the way into the Holiest,

for tearing the veil,

for revealing the Father,

and for sending the Spirit

to dwell within earthen vessels like us.

You are the Word, the Light, the Life, and the Glory revealed.

May this book magnify You more than anything else.

To the Holy Spirit,

the Spirit of Glory and the Spirit of Truth—

You were the voice behind every page,

the fire that stirred my spirit,

the comfort that sustained me,

the wisdom that guided every thought.

Without You, glory cannot be known.

Thank You for being my Teacher.

To my family,

thank you for your love, patience, and unwavering support.

You carried me in seasons of weariness

and encouraged me when the weight of the assignment felt heavy.

Your prayers, your faith, and your presence remain a vital part of this journey.

To the faithful friends and believers

who continually encourage me to pursue the deep things of God—

your hunger stirred mine.

Your passion for His presence sharpened me.

Your fellowship strengthened my hands.

To the Body of Christ,

the glorious Bride being prepared for the soon return of the King—

may these words call you deeper,

ignite your hunger,

and awaken your desire

to host His presence and walk in His glory.

To every reader who opened these pages with an open heart—

thank you.

May this book not simply inform you but transform you.

May it draw you nearer to the heart of the Father,

deepen your walk with the Holy Spirit,

and stir within you an unquenchable longing

for the glory of God.

And finally,

to all who have prayed for me, supported this work,

or stood with me in ministry—

your love is seen, your faithfulness is valued,

and your partnership is eternal.

To God be all the glory, both now and forever. Amen.

PREFACE

IN THE GLORY OF HIS PRESENCE

There are journeys we choose, and then there are journeys chosen for us by the gentle, sovereign hand of God. This book was not born from intellectual curiosity, but from a burning ache in my spirit—a longing to behold God as He truly is. For years I have read about His power, His love, and studied His word with diligence, yet I found within myself a deeper cry, a cry that echoed Moses on the mountain: "Please, show me Your glory."

We live in a generation flooded with information yet starving for revelation. Churches are filled with activity but lacking the one thing that distinguishes us from every other people on earth—the manifest presence of God. The early apostles did not turn the world upside down because of eloquence or programs. They moved in the authority of heaven because they lived in the glory of His presence. They carried something weighty, something real, something that could not be manufactured: God Himself revealed through them.

This book is a call back to that ancient path.

It is a journey into the mystery of God's glory—the weight of His essence, the radiance of His being, the overwhelming beauty of His holiness. It is a journey that begins on the fiery heights of Sinai, travels through the Tabernacle and Temple, moves into the life and ministry of Jesus Christ—the embodiment of divine glory—and continues into the outpouring of the Holy Spirit that brings us from glory to glory. It is a journey that ends not with the closing of these pages, but with a life transformed by the reality of His presence.

My desire in authoring this book is simple:

to rekindle a hunger in your heart for the God who still reveals His glory.

Not the God of theory—but the God who came down in fire, who filled the Temple until priests could not stand, who shone on the mountain until garments became like light, who tore the veil so that ordinary men and women could enter the Holy of Holies without fear.

The glory of God is not a theological idea; it is an encounter.

It is the very atmosphere of heaven, pressing upon the hearts of men. It is the weight that breaks chains, the radiance that reveals truth, the holiness that transforms, the presence that satisfies every longing the human soul carries. When the glory comes, everything that is false fades away. When the glory comes, worship becomes effortless, obedience becomes natural, and sin loses its appetite. When the glory comes, you discover what you were created for—to dwell in the presence of the One who formed you.

This book is my humble attempt to lead you into that place.

As you journey through these chapters, you will explore:

- • The meaning of God's glory in Scripture—both in Hebrew and Greek.

- • How His glory first descended on Mount Sinai.

- • What attracts His glory according to Scripture.

- • How the high priest entered the Holy of Holies as a shadow of our access in Christ.

- • Examples of God's glory throughout the Bible.

- • What causes the glory to depart—and how to restore it.

- • The fulfillment of all glory in Jesus Christ, the express image of the Father.

- • How we boldly enter His presence in the new covenant.

- • How God's glory will illuminate the new heavens and the new earth.

- • And how we can live as carriers of His glory today.

May this book not merely inform you but transform you.

May it not only teach you about His glory but draw you into it.

May every word stir a holy hunger—a desire so deep that nothing in this world can satisfy but the presence of God Himself.

My prayer is that as you read, the Holy Spirit will remove every veil from your eyes, ignite your spirit with fresh fire, and awaken in you the same cry that has followed God's people for generations:

"Lord, show me Your glory."

And may He answer you.

For to be in the glory of His presence is not only our calling—

it is our eternal destiny.

— Peter Lengwe
The Bread of Life Global Ministries

INTRODUCTION

THE HUNGER THAT DRAWS THE GLORY

There is a cry rising in the hearts of believers across the earth—a cry not born of religion or routine, but of desperation. A cry for something real. Something weighty. Something holy. A cry for the presence of God.

We live in a time when the Church has learned to function with skill, structure, and strategy. We know how to build ministries, gather crowds, and produce experiences. But there is one thing we cannot manufacture, imitate, or replace: the glory of God. Without His presence, all our efforts are empty. Without His glory, all our pursuits are powerless. Without His nearness, we may have motion, but we lack transformation.

From the beginning of Scripture to the final words of Revelation, one unbroken theme echoes through the ages:

God desires to dwell with His people.

Not at a distance. Not behind a veil. Not through intermediaries.

But with us—in glory.

This book is an invitation into that ancient longing; a longing placed in every human soul by the One who formed it. When we speak of God's glory, we speak of His very essence revealed—His weight, His fullness, His nature made known. Glory is not simply light, though it shines. It is not simply power, though it overwhelms. Glory is God Himself, manifested in a way that human beings can encounter, perceive, and be changed by.

Throughout Scripture, the glory of God is never a concept to be studied; it is a reality to be experienced. It descends, it fills, it shakes, it transforms. When the glory appears, people fall on their faces, temples tremble, mountains burn, and lives are forever altered.

Yet today, many Christians have grown content with surviving without the glory. We have settled for information without revelation, programs without presence, and worship without wonder. But something in the spirit of the remnant refuses to accept a glory-less Christianity. Something in us cries out like Moses:

"If Your Presence does not go with us, do not bring us up from here."

We were not created for a distant relationship with God.

We were created for nearness.

For communion.

For glory.

In the chapters that follow, we will trace the journey of God's glory through Scripture—

- • from Sinai's fiery summit

- • to the tabernacle and temple,

- • to the prophetic visions of Ezekiel,

- • to the incarnation of Christ, the fullness of glory in bodily form,

- • to the outpouring of the Holy Spirit who brings us into ever-increasing glory,

- • and finally, to the new heavens and new earth, where the Lamb Himself is the light.

We will explore what attracts God's glory, what causes it to depart, and what it means to live as carriers of His presence in the world today. For the question is no longer whether God desires to reveal His glory—the Scriptures testify that He does. The question is whether we will posture our hearts to receive it.

Every revival in history began with one thing: a hunger for His presence.

A people who said, "Lord, we cannot live without You."

A people who longed not just for blessings, but for the Blesser.

Not only for His gifts, but for His face.

As you read this book, may that hunger awaken in you.

May you discover that the glory of God is not reserved for the extraordinary—it is the inheritance of every believer washed in the blood of Jesus. May your heart open, your spirit become tender, and your life become a living sanctuary where the King of Glory delights to dwell.

For the purpose of this book is not to increase your knowledge.

it is to ignite your longing.

A longing that leads you—not into theology alone—but into encounter.

Not into understanding alone—but into transformation.

Not merely into reading about His glory—but into living in His glory.

May the God who revealed Himself in fire, cloud, light, and majesty…

the God whose glory filled the temple until no man could stand…

the God whose brightness shines in the face of Jesus Christ…

meet you as you turn each page.

And may your heart be forever marked by one thing:

His presence is worth everything.

Let us begin the journey—

Into the glory of His presence.

Table of Contents

ABOUT THE AUTHOR

Peter Lengwe is a passionate student of the Word of God, a teacher, and a prophetic voice dedicated to unveiling the depths of Scripture with clarity, reverence, and Holy Spirit inspiration. He writes with one consuming desire—to draw believers into a deeper encounter with the presence, power, and glory of God.

Peter's journey with the Lord has been marked by seasons of brokenness, surrender, revelation, and divine visitation. Through every chapter of his life, the Holy Spirit has shaped in him a burning hunger for truth and an unshakable conviction that God still reveals Himself to those who seek Him with their whole heart.

His books—including In the Beginning the Heavens and the Earth as Created (2022), Pierced for Our Transgressions, Mystery Babylon and World Beasts Unveiled, Fear of the Lord: The Remnant Blueprint, and many others—reflect his commitment to teaching believers how to walk in holiness, intimacy, and spiritual understanding. With each work, Peter aims to awaken the Church to her prophetic identity and to prepare a generation for the return of the King of Glory.

He is the founder of The Bread of Life Global Ministries, a ministry devoted to prayer, teaching, discipleship, and proclaiming the unchanging truth of Scripture. His writing is intentional, scripturally grounded, and spiritually stirring—designed not only to inform the mind but to transform the heart.

Peter currently resides in the United States, where he continues to write, minister, and inspire believers to pursue the presence of God with passion, purity, and unwavering faith. His desire is simple yet profound:

"That the glory of God would be revealed,

and that His people would dwell in His presence forever."

CHAPTER ONE: WHAT IS THE GLORY OF GOD? THE FULLNESS OF HIS ESSENCE

Before we can understand the journey into God's glory—how it manifests, how it transforms, how it dwells among His people—we must first understand what the Bible means when it speaks of "the glory of the LORD." Glory is not a mystical fog, nor merely an atmosphere of worship. It is not a feeling, an emotion, or an energy. The glory of God is far more profound, far more weighty, far more holy.

In Scripture, the glory of God is the revelation of His essence.

It is God making Himself known.

It is God unveiled, God revealed, God manifested in ways human beings can perceive, encounter, and respond to. When His glory appears, His character, His power, His holiness, and His presence are made undeniably real.

To understand this, we must begin where every true study of biblical concepts begins: with the original languages.

1. The Hebrew Word for Glory – Kābôd

Hebrew: דּוֹבָּכ (kābôd)

Root: kbd – to be heavy, weighty, full, abundant.

In ancient Hebrew thought, something "weighty" was significant, valuable, or honorable. Thus, kābôd carries the idea of:

- Weight – not physical, but spiritual weightiness.

- Honor – worthiness and majesty.

- Substance – something real, not imaginary.

- Splendor – visible brilliance.

- Reputation – the revealed nature of a person.

Applied to God, kābôd means:

The overwhelming weight of who God is—His being, character, power, holiness, and presence revealed and experienced by creation.

This is why Moses prayed:

"Please, show me Your glory" (Exodus 33:18).

He was not asking for light or smoke. He was asking to see God's very essence revealed. God responded by declaring His name, His character, and His goodness (Exodus 33:19; 34:5–7). The glory is inseparable from who God is.

In Scripture, God's glory is not merely seen—it is felt. It carries weight. It causes men to tremble, prophets to fall as dead, and mountains to burn.

2. The Greek Word for Glory – Doxa

Greek: δόξα (doxa)

Originally: opinion, worth, reputation.

Biblically (in the Septuagint and New Testament):

radiance, splendor, brightness, majesty, divine manifestation.

When the New Testament writers used doxa, they used it in the fully developed Hebrew sense. Thus, doxa means:

- Visible brilliance of God's presence (Luke 2:9).

- Majesty and honor belonging to God (Romans 11:36).

- The revealed nature and character of God (John 1:14).

- The shining forth of God's essence (Hebrews 1:3).

Paul speaks of:

"The light of the knowledge of the glory of God in the face of Jesus
Christ."
(2 Corinthians 4:6)

In Greek thought, doxa includes both what God is and how God reveals Himself—His brightness, His majesty, and His manifested presence.

Thus:

Kābôd reveals the weight of God's being.
Doxa reveals the radiance of God's being.
Together, they describe the same reality: God made known.

3. The Glory of God Is the Fullness of His Essence

When we speak of the "glory of God," we speak of His fullness—His very nature—breaking into our world. This is why the glory:

- Convicts' sinners (Isaiah 6).

- Transforms saints (Exodus 34:29).

- Fills temples (2 Chronicles 5:14).

- Guides His people (Exodus 40:36–38).

- Reveals His holiness (Leviticus 9:24).

- Announces His presence (Ezekiel 1:28).

- Shines through Jesus Christ (John 1:14).

- Dwells in believers today (Colossians 1:27).

In its simplest form:

The glory is God Himself revealed—God stepping out of the invisible into the visible.

Everything God is—His love, His holiness, His power, His wisdom, His mercy—shines out in His glory.

This is why the psalmist declares:

"The heavens declare the glory of God" (Psalm 19:1)—
creation is the revelation of His nature.
And why Isaiah saw the seraphim cry:
"The whole earth is full of His glory!" (Isaiah 6:3)—
because every part of creation bears witness to who He is.

4. The Glory Is the Mark of God's Presence

Throughout Scripture, whenever God draws near, the glory appears.

The glory is His signature—the evidence of His presence.

- Adam and Eve walked in His glory in the Garden before the fall.

- Israel saw His glory in cloud and fire.

- The priests could not stand when the glory filled the Temple.

- Jesus revealed the glory of the Father in human flesh.

- The early Church walked in resurrection glory through the Spirit.

- The new earth will be illuminated by the glory of God.

The glory is God's way of saying:

"I am here."

It is His nearness unveiled.

His holiness revealed.

His beauty disclosed.

His heartbeat made known.

5. The Glory Is the Destiny of Every Believer

God did not save us only to forgive us; He saved us to bring us into His presence, into fellowship with Him, into His glory.

Paul writes:

"Christ in you, the hope of glory." (Colossians 1:27)

And again:

"We... are being transformed into the same image from glory to glory."
(2 Corinthians 3:18)

Our destiny is not religion—

our destiny is glory.

We were made for His presence.

We were formed to carry His likeness.

We were created to live in His radiance.

This is the essence of eternal life:

not merely living forever, but living with Him, surrounded by the brilliance of His glory.

Closing Prayer

Father, reveal to us the glory of who You are.

Remove every veil from our eyes and every distraction from our hearts.

Let us behold the beauty, the holiness, and the weight of Your presence.

Teach us to recognize Your glory, to honor Your glory,

and to walk in the fullness of Your essence.

May Your Spirit open our understanding

so that this journey becomes more than knowledge—

let it become encounter.

Draw us into deeper hunger, deeper reverence,

and deeper longing for the God of glory.

In Jesus' mighty name, Amen.

CHAPTER TWO: WHEN GLORY CAME DOWN: THE FIRST DESCENT ON SINAI

Before the tabernacle.

Before the Temple.

Before the priests and sacrifices.

God chose a mountain—a mountain of stone, dust, and desert winds—to reveal His glory to a nation He had just redeemed from slavery. This was not a soft moment of quiet revelation. This was the God of heaven stepping into the earth with undeniable, terrifying majesty.

Sinai was not simply a mountain.

Sinai was the throne of God touching the earth.

It was there that the glory of God descended for the first time before the eyes of the entire nation of Israel. A moment so powerful that Scripture says the people stood at a distance, trembling, begging Moses to speak to God on their behalf.

For at Sinai, the invisible God made Himself visible.

The God who spoke from burning bushes now spoke from a burning mountain.

The God who led by cloud and fire now rested upon a summit in fire and glory.

This was a revelation of His holiness, His power, and His unapproachable majesty.

1. The Setting of Sinai: A Holy Summons

After delivering Israel from Egypt by signs and wonders, God led them to "the mountain of God" (Exodus 3:12). This was not accidental. Sinai was the destination of their redemption. Freedom from bondage was not the end—the presence of God was the end.

God told Moses:

"You shall be to Me a kingdom of priests and a holy nation."
(Exodus 19:6)

Before giving them laws, before forming rituals, before establishing worship, God revealed His glory. He did not invite them into religion; He invited them into relationship—a relationship marked by His presence.

When Israel arrived at Sinai, God instructed Moses to sanctify the people for two days. Why?

Because the glory was coming down.

He was teaching them a pattern:

Holiness prepares the heart for His presence.

2. The Descent of His Glory

On the third day, the heavens responded.

Exodus 19 describes the scene:

- Thunder and lightning split the sky.

- A thick cloud covered the mountain.

- A trumpet blast grew louder and louder, though no human blew it.

- The entire mountain trembled violently.

- Fire descended and smoke billowed "like the smoke of a furnace."

- And the Lord descended in glory and flame.

This was no ordinary event.

This was no symbolic vision.

This was the literal, manifested glory of the Living God, the Creator of heaven and earth.

Moses wrote:

"The sight of the glory of the LORD was like a consuming fire on the top of the mountain."
(Exodus 24:17)

To the Israelites, the glory was not gentle—it was overwhelming. It pressed on their senses with such intensity that they trembled and backed away. They begged Moses:

"You speak with us... but let not God speak with us, lest we die."
(Exodus 20:19)

Why?

Because when the glory comes, the human soul is confronted with the full reality of God's holiness.

Sinai teaches us that God's glory is beautiful, but it is also terrifying to the flesh. It exposes every impurity. It reveals the distance between humanity and divine perfection. Yet it also calls the heart upward—toward reverence, worship, and surrender.

3. Sinai's Glory Revealed God's Nature

The descent on Sinai was not simply a display of power; it was a revelation of who God is.

A God of Holiness

Sinai was fenced off. No one could touch it.

Holiness is not casual; it demands reverence.

A God of Order

Everything—from the preparation of the people to the boundaries around the mountain—reflected divine order. Glory comes where God's order is honored.

A God of Covenant

Before the commandments were given, the glory appeared. God was showing that the law flows from His nature. His glory came before His instructions.

A God of Manifest Presence

He is not distant.

He is not silent.

He is a God who comes down.

4. The Mountain That Trembled Points to the God Who Draws Near

Sinai was a moment of divine confrontation—but also divine invitation.

The God who descended in fire also said:

"I bore you on eagles' wings and brought you to Myself."
(Exodus 19:4)

God did not bring Israel to Sinai to terrify them.

He brought them to reveal the glory of the One who had redeemed them.

He brought them to show that they were now His people, His inheritance, His priesthood.

Sinai was both the fear of the Lord and the love of the Lord displayed together.

The fear of the Lord—because His glory is not to be treated lightly.

The love of the Lord—because His glory comes to dwell among those, He has called His own.

5. Sinai Foreshadows the Glory to Come

Sinai was a beginning, not an end. It pointed forward to something greater:

- The glories of the Tabernacle and Temple.

- Ezekiel's visions of the heavenly throne.

- The incarnation of Jesus, "the glory of the Only Begotten of the Father."

- The transfiguration on the mountain where His glory shone like the sun.

- The outpouring of the Spirit at Pentecost—fire once again descending on the people of God.

- The New Covenant invitation into the Holy of Holies.

- And, the New Jerusalem, lit forever by the glory of God.

Hebrews 12:18–24 compares Sinai with Zion, showing that Sinai was only the shadow of the glory believers now access through Christ.

At Sinai, the people could not come near.

At Zion, the people are invited to draw near.

At Sinai, the mountain burned with fire.

At Pentecost, the fire came upon each believer.

At Sinai, only Moses could ascend.

At Zion, every believer is seated with Christ in heavenly places.

The glory that terrified Israel is the same glory believers now approach with boldness—

because of the blood of the Lamb.

Closing Prayer

Father, thank You for revealing Yourself at Sinai.

Thank You for showing us the holiness, majesty, and reality of Your presence.

Teach us to honor Your glory with reverence,

to prepare our hearts as Israel prepared themselves,

and to seek Your face with humility and awe.

Let the fire that descended on Sinai awaken a fresh fear of the Lord within us,

and let that holy fear lead us into deeper intimacy with You.

As we journey further in this book,

may Your Spirit draw us closer to the God who reveals His glory.

In Jesus' name, Amen.

CHAPTER THREE: PATTERNS OF HIS GLORY: THE TABERNACLE, THE TEMPLE, AND THE HIGH PRIEST

When the glory descended on Sinai, God did not intend it to be a one-time encounter. The fire on the mountain was the beginning of a divine blueprint—a heavenly pattern meant to teach Israel (and us) how to approach the Holy One in a way that honors His nature. From Sinai, God began to reveal the design through which His glory would dwell among His people continuously. This pattern took shape in the Tabernacle, was expanded in the Temple, and found fulfillment in the ministry of the High Priest.

Through these three divine structures, God taught Israel how His presence is approached, how His glory is sustained, and how the human heart becomes a dwelling place for God Himself.

1. "Build According to the Pattern": A Heavenly Blueprint

After Sinai, God instructed Moses:

"Let them make Me a sanctuary, that I may dwell among them.
According to all that I show you, that is, the pattern…"
(Exodus 25:8–9)

The word pattern (Hebrew: tabnith) means a heavenly model, a divine blueprint shown by God. Moses was not permitted to build according to his own creative ability. The tabernacle was not a man-designed place of worship; it was a God-designed dwelling of glory.

This truth reveals a profound principle:

God's glory rests only where God's order is honored.

The tabernacle was arranged in three distinct zones:

1. The Outer Court – sacrifice and cleansing.

2. The Holy Place – fellowship and ministry.

3. The Holy of Holies – the throne room of God.

Each area represented a step deeper into the presence of God, teaching that approaching His glory requires alignment with His ways.

2. The Outer Court: Atonement Before Access

The first thing a worshiper saw upon entering the tabernacle was the Brazen Altar, a place of sacrifice and blood. No one drew near to God without passing by the altar. This taught Israel:

*   Sin must be dealt with.

*   A substitute must die for the guilty to approach God.

- The glory cannot dwell where the guilt of sin remains.

Right after the altar stood the Bronze Laver, a basin for washing. The priests washed not because they were dirty in the physical sense, but because God is holy, and everything that touches His presence must be cleansed.

The outer court screamed a single message:

No man enters the presence of God without sacrifice and cleansing.

This was a shadow of the cross—

the once-for-all sacrifice that grants us entrance into His glory today.

3. The Holy Place: Worship, Light, and Fellowship

Only priestly ministry took place in the Holy Place. Here stood:

The Golden Lampstand

Representing:

- The light of revelation

- The illumination of the Spirit

- The continual shining presence of God

The Table of Showbread

Symbolizing:

- Fellowship

- Communion

- God providing His presence as nourishment

The Altar of Incense

A picture of:

- Worship

- Intercession

- The prayers of the saints rising before God

In this room, the atmosphere changed. The worshiper had moved from dealing with sin to ministering to God. This was no longer the realm of guilt; it was the realm of relationship.

But beyond the Holy Place lay something even greater…

4. The Holy of Holies: The Dwelling of His Glory

Separated by a thick veil, the Holy of Holies was the most sacred space on earth. Inside was the Ark of the Covenant, and on top of it the Mercy Seat, overshadowed by golden cherubim.

This was the throne of God on earth.

Here, the glory of the Lord dwelt.

Here, the Shekinah filled the room with light.

Here, heaven and earth met.

The Holy of Holies teaches us:

- The glory is relational—God dwells among His people.

- The glory is exclusive—God determines how He is approached.

- The glory is holy—not to be taken lightly or entered casually.

Only one man—the High Priest—entered this place.

And only once per year.

And only with blood.

5. The High Priest: The Shadow of Access into Glory

The High Priest's yearly entrance on the Day of Atonement (Leviticus 16) is one of the most powerful pictures of approaching God's glory.

He entered with:

- Garments of purity

- Blood of sacrifice

- Incense to cloud the mercy seat

- Bells on his robe so the people could hear him moving

- A rope, according to Jewish tradition, so his body could be removed if he died inside the glory

Every detail taught a spiritual truth:

A. Only the appointed priest can enter the glory

He was chosen by God, not by men.

B. Only blood grants access

Without the shedding of blood, there is no approach to God.

C. Only holiness sustains one in the glory

Unholiness in God's presence leads to death.

D. Access is costly

The priest's garments, sacrifices, and rituals all proclaimed the weight of God's holiness.

E. The High Priest was a foreshadowing of Christ

Hebrews 9 reveals that Jesus is:

- The true High Priest

- Who entered not an earthly tabernacle

- But the heavenly Holy of Holies

- With His own blood

- To obtain eternal redemption

- Opening the way for all believers to enter the glory

The earthly priesthood showed the barrier.

Christ removed the barrier.

The earthly veil hid God's glory.

Christ tore the veil.

The earthly sanctuary limited access.

Christ opened unlimited access.

6. The Tabernacle and Temple Show God's Desire to Dwell Among Us

The most important truth revealed through these patterns is this:

God longs to dwell with His people.

The tabernacle was mobile—God moving with His people.

The temple was permanent—God dwelling among His people.

Both pointed forward to:

- Christ, the true temple (John 2:21)

- The believer, the living temple (1 Corinthians 3:16)

- The Church, the holy dwelling of God (Ephesians 2:22)

- The New Jerusalem, where God dwells with man forever (Revelation 21:3)

The glory that descended on Sinai did not remain on a mountain.

It followed Israel into the tabernacle.

It filled Solomon's temple.

It came in the flesh in Jesus Christ.

It came in fire at Pentecost.

And it will one day fill all creation.

God has always desired not visits—

but habitation.

Closing Prayer

Father, thank You for revealing the pattern of Your glory through the tabernacle, the temple, and the ministry of the High Priest.

Teach us to honor Your order, to walk in holiness, and to seek Your presence with reverence.

Remove every veil from our hearts and draw us deeper into Your dwelling place.

May we become living temples where Your glory rests.

And through Jesus, our true High Priest, grant us bold access into the Holy of Holies.

Let Your presence become our home, our desire, and our delight.

In Jesus' mighty name, Amen.

CHAPTER FOUR: WHAT BRINGS THE GLORY OF GOD: HOLINESS, UNITY, WORSHIP, AND OBEDIENCE

The glory of God does not appear randomly. It is not drawn by emotion, atmosphere, or human effort. Throughout Scripture, the glory of God responds to conditions—divine patterns that attract His presence and prepare a place for Him to dwell. God is sovereign in revealing His glory, but He also reveals that He draws near where His nature is honored.

In the Bible, there are four foundational pillars that consistently precede manifestations of God's glory:

1. Holiness

2.   Unity

3.   Worship

4.   Obedience

Where these four are cultivated, His glory comes.

Where these are absent, His glory departs.

In this chapter we examine these pillars through the lens of Scripture, particularly 2 Chronicles 5:14 and Psalm 15, two of the clearest pictures of what attracts the weight of His presence.

1. Holiness: The Foundation of His Glory

Holiness is not optional for encountering God's presence; it is essential. God's glory rests only where His nature is honored.

Psalm 15 asks:

> *"LORD, who may abide in Your tabernacle?*
> *Who may dwell in Your holy hill?"*
> *(Psalm 15:1)*

The answer reveals the character required for those who would carry His presence:

- He who walks uprightly

- Speaks truth in his heart

- Does not slander

- Does no evil to his neighbor

- Honors those who fear the Lord

- Keeps his word

- Refuses bribes and corruption

This is a portrait of a heart and life aligned with God's holiness.

The glory of God does not rest where sin is celebrated, where compromise is embraced, or where flesh governs. Holiness is not perfection—but purity of heart, sincerity of devotion, and separation unto God.

Holiness attracts glory because:

- It reflects God's nature.

- It prepares the vessel.

- It removes what hinders His presence.

- It honors the throne of God.

The glory that fell at Sinai and filled the Temple only rested where God's people were set apart for Him.

2. Unity: One Sound That Invites the Presence

One of the most powerful scenes of glory in Scripture occurs in 2 Chronicles 5:11–14, during the dedication of Solomon's Temple.

The priests and Levites assembled in unity, and Scripture says:

"...the trumpeters and singers were as one,
to make one sound to be heard in praising and thanking the LORD..."
(2 Chronicles 5:13)

When they lifted their voices in one accord, declaring:

"For He is good, and His mercy endures forever,"

the glory of the Lord filled the house so powerfully that:

"...the priests could not stand to minister because of the cloud..."
(v.14)

Unity releases the atmosphere in which the glory descends.

Not unity of personality, but unity of purpose, heart, and worship.

Unity attracts glory because:

- It reflects the oneness of God's nature.

- It dismantles pride and self-promotion.

- It aligns earth with the unity of heaven.

- It creates a place where God commands blessing (Psalm 133).

The early church in Acts 2 was "in one accord" when the Spirit came as a rushing mighty wind. Glory rests where God's people move as one.

3. Worship: The Environment of His Presence

Worship is the language of glory.

Where true worship rises, the presence responds.

In 2 Chronicles 5:14, the glory descended in direct response to the worship of God's people. Not performance. Not entertainment.

Pure, unified, God-centered worship.

Their words were simple:

"For He is good, for His mercy endures forever."

Worship in Scripture is always:

- God-focused

- Truth-centered

- Reverent

- Sacrificial

- Filled with gratitude and wonder

Worship invites the glory because it enthrones God:

> *"You are holy, enthroned in the praises of Israel."*
> *(Psalm 22:3)*

Worship shifts the atmosphere from earth to heaven, causing the weight of His presence to descend.

When Solomon worshipped, glory came.

When Jehoshaphat worshipped, victory came.

When Paul and Silas worshipped, chains broke.

When the early church worshipped, places were shaken.

Worship doesn't move God—

worship aligns us with where God already is.

4. Obedience: The Pathway That Sustains the Glory

Obedience is the evidence of love and the foundation of divine habitation.

Jesus said:

> *"If anyone loves Me, he will keep My word... and We will come to him*
> *and make Our home with him."*
> *(John 14:23)*

Disobedience drives away the presence, but obedience opens the door to God's dwelling.

Throughout the tabernacle and Temple narrative, glory always followed obedience:

- Moses built "according to the pattern."
  The glory came (Exodus 40:34–38).

- Solomon built exactly as instructed.
  The glory filled the house (2 Chronicles 7:1–3).

- The early church obeyed the command to wait in Jerusalem.
  The Spirit descended in glory (Acts 2:1–4).

Obedience is not legalism—it is alignment with God's ways so His presence can rest upon us without hindrance.

Obedience attracts glory because:

- It honors God's authority.

- It removes spiritual resistance.

- It demonstrates trust.

- It creates stability for God's dwelling.

Where obedience is practiced, glory remains.

5. When All Four Come Together, the Glory Falls

When holiness, unity, worship, and obedience converge, the atmosphere becomes a resting place for His presence.

This is why:

- Sinai shook.

- The tabernacle filled with cloud.

- The temple was overwhelmed with glory.

- Pentecost exploded in fire.

- The early church walked in miracles, boldness, and fear of the Lord.

God has not changed.

His patterns have not changed.

The same conditions that brought the glory in Scripture bring it today.

He still responds to:

- Holiness of heart

- Unity of spirit

- Worship of truth

- Obedience of faith

Where these are honored, His glory comes.

Closing Prayer

Father, teach us the ways that attract Your glory.

Cleanse our hearts that we may walk in holiness.

Bind us together in unity, as one body and one spirit.

Awaken true worship within us, worship that honors Your name.

Give us obedient hearts that delight to follow Your ways.

Prepare us as vessels of Your presence,

that the glory that filled the Temple may fill our lives.

Draw us deeper into alignment with heaven,

so that Your glory may rest and remain upon us.

In Jesus' mighty name, Amen.

CHAPTER FIVE: BIBLICAL PORTRAITS OF THE GLORY OF GOD

From Genesis to Revelation, God has painted portraits of His glory across the pages of His Word. These portraits are not merely historical events; they are revelations of God's nature—snapshots of His presence breaking into the human realm. Each moment teaches us something unique about the character, power, and holiness of God.

In this chapter, we will walk through some of the most significant manifestations of His glory, allowing Scripture to reveal the many dimensions of the God who dwells in unapproachable light yet chooses to make Himself known to His people.

1. Moses and the Shining Face — The Glory That Transforms

(Exodus 34:29–35)

After spending forty days and nights in the presence of God on Mount

Sinai, Moses descended with the tablets of the covenant. Scripture says:

"The skin of his face shone while he talked with Him."

Moses did not even realize what had happened—transformation had taken place simply by being in the glory.

Key Revelation:

The glory of God transforms those who behold it.

Moses reflected the glory the way the moon reflects the light of the sun. This was not an external anointing—this was internal transformation. The glory marked him visibly, tangibly, undeniably.

This is a prophetic picture of what Paul spoke when he declared:

"We... beholding as in a mirror the glory of the Lord, are being transformed into the same image from glory to glory."
(2 Corinthians 3:18)

Those who dwell in His presence do not leave the same.

2. The Dedication of Solomon's Temple — The Glory That Fills and Overwhelms

(2 Chronicles 7:1–3)

When Solomon completed the temple according to God's pattern, Scripture records a dramatic moment:

- Fire fell from heaven, consuming the burnt offering.

- The glory of the Lord filled the house.

- The priests could not enter because the weight of His presence was overwhelming.

- All Israel bowed with their faces to the ground.

The people responded with a single declaration:

"For He is good, for His mercy endures forever!"

Key Revelation:

When God's glory comes, human strength fails and worship erupts.

The glory took over the atmosphere. Ministry ceased. No one could stand. God Himself ministered to His people.

The temple dedication teaches that:

- God confirms what is built according to His pattern.

- His glory comes where sacrifice and worship align.

- His presence is more powerful than any human effort.

3. Ezekiel's Visions of the Glory — The Glory That Reveals the Throne of God

(Ezekiel chapters 1 & 10)

No prophet saw the glory as vividly as Ezekiel. While exiled in Babylon, he saw visions that revealed the heavenly realm:

- Living creatures with four faces.

- Wheels within wheels.

- Lightning, fire, and brightness all around.

- A throne of sapphire above the expanse.

- And One seated on the throne, radiant like fire and light.

When Ezekiel saw this, he fell on his face.

He described the vision as:

"The appearance of the likeness of the glory of the LORD."
(Ezekiel 1:28)

Later, Ezekiel saw the heartbreaking opposite—the glory departing from the temple because of Israel's sin (Ezekiel 10–11).

Key Revelation:

God's glory is connected to His throne—His sovereign rule and holy presence.
And sin drives His glory away.

Through Ezekiel's visions, we learn:

- The glory is majestic beyond expression.

- The glory is the center of all heavenly activity.

- The glory reveals the holiness and kingship of God.

- The glory departs when God's people embrace idolatry and rebellion.

Ezekiel gives us both the wonder of His presence and the warning of losing it.

4. The Transfiguration of Jesus — The Glory Revealed in the Son

(Matthew 17:1–8, Mark 9:2–8, Luke 9:28–36)

On a high mountain, Jesus took Peter, James, and John and was transfigured before them.

Scripture says:

- His face shone like the sun.

- His clothes became white as light.

- Moses and Elijah appeared, testifying to Him.

- A bright cloud overshadowed them.

- A voice spoke:
  "This is My beloved Son, in whom I am well pleased. Hear Him!"

This was not a borrowed glory—

this was the eternal glory of the Son of God breaking through His humanity.

Key Revelation:

Jesus Christ is the ultimate revelation of the glory of God.

What Moses reflected, Jesus radiates.

What the prophets saw in part, Jesus embodies in full.

The disciples witnessed:

- The glory of His deity.

- The glory of His authority.

- The glory of His identity as the Son.

And after the vision, Jesus touched them and said:

"Do not be afraid."

The One who reveals glory also grants peace.

5. The Early Church — The Glory That Empowers, Fills, and Shakes

(Acts 2–7)

The glory did not remain in temples or on mountains.

Through the Holy Spirit, it entered the believers themselves.

Pentecost (Acts 2)

- A sound like a rushing mighty wind.

- Flames of fire resting on each believer.

- Bold preaching.

- Supernatural utterance.

- Thousands saved.

Acts 4

- The place where they gathered shook.

- They were filled with boldness.

- Great power and great grace rested upon them.

Acts 7

Stephen, filled with the Holy Spirit, gazed into heaven, and saw the glory of God, and Jesus standing at the right hand of God.

Key Revelation:

The glory of God is not limited to structures—it now lives in His people.

The early church operated in:

- Power

- Unity

- Fear of the Lord

- Miracles

- Boldness

- Overflowing grace

They were walking embodiments of the glory of God on the earth.

6. What These Portraits Reveal About the Glory of God

Throughout these encounters, we see consistent truths:

A. The glory transforms.

Moses' face shone. Lives were changed.

B. The glory fills environments.

Temples, upper rooms, and even prisons.

C. The glory reveals Christ.

From the transfiguration to Stephen's vision.

D. The glory empowers believers.

Pentecost and the early church.

E. The glory departs when God is dishonored.

Ezekiel's vision of Ichabod over the temple.

F. The glory is God's chosen way to reveal Himself.

Fire, cloud, light, voice, throne, and the Son.

Every portrait is a window into the eternal nature of the God who desires to dwell with His people.

Closing Prayer

Father, thank You for every revelation of Your glory throughout Scripture.

Thank You for the portraits that show us Your holiness, Your power, and Your love.

Open our eyes to behold Your glory as Moses did,

to worship like Israel did,

to stand in awe like Ezekiel,

to see Jesus lifted high like the disciples on the mount,

and to walk in the power of the Spirit as the early church did.

Let these portraits ignite in us a deeper hunger for Your presence.

Transform us from glory to glory as we behold Your face.

In Jesus' mighty name, Amen.

**CHAPTER SIX:
THE COST OF LIVING
OUTSIDE THE GLORY:
THE THEOLOGY OF WHAT
REMOVES GOD'S GLORY**

The glory of God—kābôd (Hebrew: כ ּ דוב), meaning weight, heaviness, honor, abundance, splendor—is not merely a divine emotion. It is the manifest essence of God's being dwelling among His people. In the New Testament, the glory becomes dóxa (δόξα), meaning radiance, reputation, divine majesty revealed.

When God's glory is present, His nature is visible, His kingdom is active, and His presence is tangible.

But when His glory departs, the absence is not silence—it is judgment.

The departure of glory (Ichabod) is never arbitrary. It is always the result of a breach in covenantal alignment, a violation of spiritual law, or the defilement of sacred space.

This chapter unveils the theological laws governing the presence of God and the conditions that cause the glory to lift.

1. SIN: THE COVENANT BREAKER AND GLORY DIMMER

Sin is not merely moral failure; it is treason against divine order.

In Hebrew, the primary terms for sin—

- chattā' (אָטַח): to miss the mark

- pāshaʿ (עָשֶׁפ): rebellion

- ʿāwōn (וֹוָע): twistedness, iniquity

—describe violations not only of God's commands but of His nature.

Sin disfigures the image of God in man; therefore, it repels the glory of God from man.

Paul writes:

"...all have sinned and fall short (hysteréō—be destitute, lack) of the glory of God."
— Romans 3:23 (NKJV)

This means sin robs man of the capacity to host glory. It is not simply that God removes glory; it is that man becomes spiritually incompatible with it.

Sin introduced shame, and shame replaced splendor.

Adam was clothed with glory, but after sin he became conscious of nakedness—the stripping of divine covering.

Wherever sin reigns, glory cannot abide.

2. PRIDE: THE ORIGINAL GLORY-THIEF AND THE NATURE OF SATAN

Pride is not merely arrogance—it is the desire to possess glory without God.

It was pride that transformed Hêlel ben Shachar (רֹחַשְׁ-וּבָ לְלֵיהֶ)—the shining one, "Lucifer"—into Satan.

"I will ascend...I will exalt...I will sit...I will be like the Most High."
— Isaiah 14:13–14

This was a direct attempt to usurp divine glory rather than reflect it.

Pride caused the first glory departure in history: the exile of Lucifer from heaven.

Where pride operates, Satan's nature is present—and God's glory refuses fellowship with darkness.

James affirms a spiritual law:

"God resists the proud..."
— James 4:6

The word antitássō (ἀντιτάσσω) means "to set oneself in battle array against."

Pride does not merely hinder glory; it places God in opposition to the proud heart.

3. REBELLION: VIOLATION OF DIVINE ORDER AND PRIESTHOOD

Rebellion is fundamentally anti-priesthood because it circumvents divine authority.

In Scripture, rebellion is likened to witchcraft (1 Samuel 15:23)—not figuratively but theologically. Witchcraft seeks spiritual power without submission; rebellion seeks glory without obedience.

Saul's partial obedience was covenant violation; therefore, the glory manifested as kingship was taken:

"The LORD has torn the kingdom from you."

The kingdom operates by divine order; rebellion is an inversion of divine order. It breaks the alignment that glory requires.

4. UNBELIEF: THE BLOCKADE OF DIVINE MANIFESTATION

In Greek, unbelief is apistía (ἀπιστία)—a refusal to be persuaded.

Unbelief isn't intellectual doubt; it is spiritual resistance to the revelation of God.

In Nazareth:

"He could do no mighty work there because of their unbelief."
— Mark 6:5–6

This does not imply weakness in Christ but the spiritual law that glory requires a vessel of faith.

Faith is the atmosphere of glory.

Unbelief is the vacuum of glory.

Unbelief shuts the gates of manifestation, making divine activity legally restricted by the hardened condition of the human heart.

5. IDOLATRY: THE RIVAL HOST OF THE GLORY

God's glory is jealous—not in insecurity but in covenantal exclusivity.

"My glory I will not give to another."
— Isaiah 42:8

Idolatry—Hebrew: ʿāven, pesel, bāmâ—is the enthronement of anything above God:

- self

- ministry

- relationships

- money

- traditions

- systems

- spiritual gifts

- religious pride

When Eli's sons corrupted the priesthood, the ark was taken, and Ichabod was declared.

The ark represented God's throne, the place of glory.

Pollute the throne, and the glory withdraws.

Where idols stand, God's glory does not.

6. DEFILEMENT OF SACRED SPACE

The temple—whether in Jerusalem or the believer—must be consecrated.

Paul writes:

> *"You are the temple of the Holy Spirit."*
> *— 1 Corinthians 6:19*

If the temple becomes polluted through:

- sexual immorality

- occult practices

- mixture

- unclean spiritual influences

- profanity of worship

- misaligned motives

—then the glory lifts because God will not share holy space with corruption.

In Ezekiel 8–10, the glory departs the temple progressively because of abominations committed in its courts.

This shows the terrifying theological truth:

Glory does not leave suddenly; it leaves step by step.

7. DISUNITY: THE DISMANTLING OF CORPORATE GLORY

Glory has both individual and corporate dimensions.

At Solomon's temple dedication:

> *"…the glory of the LORD filled the house."*
> *— 2 Chronicles 5:14*

But this glory descended after the people became one:

> *"…the Levites stood as one…" (v. 13, Hebrew: echad, אחד — unified, woven together)*

Division is not merely relational tension; it is spiritual disintegration of the dwelling place of God.

A divided people cannot host a unified glory.

8. RELIGIOUS FORM WITHOUT PRESENCE: EMPTY ARK, EMPTY ALTAR

God never honors a system void of His Spirit.

The Pharisees had Torah, tradition, sacrifice, structure—and yet Jesus said:

> *"…you are whitewashed tombs…"*

Religion without glory is a graveyard of rituals.

Paul describes it:

> *"…having a form of godliness but denying its power."*
> *— 2 Timothy 3:5*

Form without presence is an affront to God because it imitates the appearance of holiness while rejecting the substance of holiness.

Glory cannot rest on pretense.

9. FEAR OF MAN: THE MISPLACED REVERENCE THAT EXPELS GLORY

The fear of the Lord attracts glory; fear of man expels it.

Saul said:

> *"…I feared the people and obeyed their voice."*
> *— 1 Samuel 15:24*

This is theological:

Fear is a form of worship.

Whatever you fear, you exalt.

Whatever you exalt, you enthrone.

Whatever you enthrone governs your life.

If the opinions of people are enthroned, the glory is dethroned.

10. NEGLECT OF DIVINE PRESENCE: THE DIMMING OF SACRED FIRE

God commanded the priests:

"The fire shall ever be burning on the altar; it shall never go out."
— *Leviticus 6:13*

The fire represents His presence.

Neglect is a slow extinguishing of the flame.

When spiritual disciplines fade:

- prayer weakens

- worship becomes mechanical

- the Word becomes distant

- repentance becomes infrequent

- holiness is devalued

—then the fire dims.

Not because God withdraws suddenly, but because the human heart ceases to host Him.

The glory lifts when its altar is abandoned.

THE THEOLOGICAL HOPE: GOD RESTORES GLORY TO THE REPENTANT

The glory departs legally—but it returns mercifully.

When the temple was cleansed under Hezekiah, the glory returned.

When Israel repented under Samuel, the ark returned.

When Christ was resurrected, the veil was torn, and glory became accessible to all who believe.

The theological pattern is always the same:

Repentance → Consecration → Realignment → Restoration of Glory

The glory is not fragile;

It is holy.

It is not temperamental;

It is righteous.

It does not flee from weakness;

It flees from corruption.

Whenever a heart, a home, or a people rediscover the fear of the Lord, humility, worship, and obedience—the glory comes again.

**CHAPTER SIX:
THE LOSS OF GLORY: THE THEOLOGY OF WHAT CAUSES GOD'S GLORY TO DEPART**

The glory of God—kābôd (Hebrew דּוֹב ֶכּ): weight, substance, splendor, heaviness of divine reality—is not merely an atmosphere or sensation. It is the self-disclosure of God's holy essence, His radiance made visible, His presence made experiential.

In Greek, dóxa (δόξα) means majesty, brilliance, divine manifestation.

Glory is not optional in the life of God's people; it is the sign that God Himself is dwelling among them.

Where the glory is, the kingdom is active.

Where the glory is absent, judgment is operating—even if silently.

The glory never departs without cause.

It withdraws according to laws, patterns, and covenant principles woven from Genesis to Revelation.

Understanding these laws is essential because God's glory is both the highest calling and the most easily forfeited treasure.

This chapter reveals the spiritual mechanics, theological foundations, and biblical precedents of why the glory of God lifts from a life, a ministry, a nation, or a generation.

1. SIN: THE PRIMARY BREACH OF COVENANT AND THE FIRST GLORY-REMOVER

Sin is not merely moral wrongdoing; it is covenant violation at its most fundamental level.

In Hebrew Scripture, sin appears in three main forms:

1. "Chattā'" (אטָח)

– missing the mark, deviating from divine order

2. "Pesha'" (עֶשֶׁפָּ)

– rebellion against divine authority

3. "'Āwon" (וֹעָו)

– iniquity, twistedness, corruption of nature

These are not merely actions—they are states of being that repel the presence of God because they contradict His nature.

Adam lost the glory because sin altered his nature.

He was created to host glory—but sin made him spiritually

incompatible with it.

Paul later confirms this cosmic reality:

"...all have sinned and fall short (hysteréō) of the glory of God."
— *Romans 3:23 (NKJV)*

Sin diminishes the capacity of the human vessel to carry divine weight.

Where sin is celebrated, defended, or excused, the glory cannot remain.

2. PRIDE: THE ORIGINAL SIN THAT REMOVED GLORY FROM HEAVEN

Before sin entered humanity, it entered the spiritual realm.

Lucifer, the "shining one" (Hêlel ben Shachar, Isa. 14), was adorned with glory (Ezek. 28:12–15). His fall reveals the first theological law of glory:

Pride is the attempt to possess glory rather than reflect it.

Pride desires God's prerogatives without God's nature.

It seeks God's throne without God's character.

"I will ascend... I will exalt... I will sit... I will be like the Most High."
— *Isaiah 14:13–14*

These five "I wills" represent the anti-glory posture.

Therefore:

Pride expelled Lucifer from the glory realm

—and pride continues to expel glory from lives, churches, and nations.

James writes:

"God resists the proud..."
— James 4:6

Antitássō (ἀντιτάσσω) means God actively opposes the proud.

If God is resisting someone, His glory certainly is not resting upon them.

3. REBELLION: THE THEOLOGICAL EQUIVALENT OF WITCHCRAFT

Rebellion is not misbehavior—it is spiritual mutiny.

The Hebrew word pasha' means "to break away from authority."

In 1 Samuel 15, Saul partially obeys but spiritually rebels. This reveals another divine law:

Partial obedience is still rebellion in the realm of glory.

Samuel declares:

"Rebellion is as the sin of witchcraft."
— 1 Samuel 15:23

Why witchcraft?

Because both rebellion and witchcraft seek spiritual influence apart from divine order.

Rebellion dethrones God in the heart.

Thus, the glory leaves because it refuses to abide where self-rule prevails.

4. IDOLATRY: THE GLORY-RIVAL AND COVENANT VIOLATION

God warns repeatedly:

"My glory I will not give to another."
— Isaiah 42:8

Idolatry is not only bowing to statues; it is the enthronement of anything that competes for the heart's affection, including:

- ambition

- relationships

- titles

- ministry

- money

- religious systems

- self

When Eli's sons polluted the priesthood, Israel went to battle without holiness and expected victory. The ark was taken, and the glory departed. A child was named:

Ichabod — "The glory has departed."

Where idols stand—whether visible or hidden—the glory withdraws.

5. DEFILEMENT OF THE TEMPLE: POLLUTING THE DWELLING PLACE OF GOD

Temple theology is essential because God's glory is tied to sacred space.

There are three temples in Scripture:

1. The heavenly temple—God's eternal dwelling

2. The earthly temple/tabernacle—the physical type

3. The believer's body—the New Covenant temple (1 Cor. 6:19)

Defilement occurs when what is holy is polluted by:

- sexual immorality

- occult involvement

- mixture

- unclean spiritual atmospheres

- dishonor

- unforgiveness

- secret sin

Ezekiel 8–10 shows the most terrifying progression in Scripture:

the slow, step-by-step departure of the glory.

The glory moves:

1. From the cherubim

2. To the threshold

3. To the east gate

4. To the mountain

5. And then gone

This shows the seriousness of defilement:

God's glory leaves gradually… not suddenly.

People often don't notice until it is gone.

6. UNBELIEF AND HARDNESS OF HEART: BLOCKING DIVINE MANIFESTATION

Unbelief is apistía (ἀπιστία)—a refusal to be convinced.

It is not intellectual doubt; it is spiritual stubbornness.

Jesus "could do no mighty works" in Nazareth because unbelief created a legal barrier in the spiritual realm.

Faith attracts glory; unbelief repels it.

A hardened heart becomes resistant to divine impressions, unable to discern God's movements.

Where unbelief rules, glory cannot manifest.

7. DISUNITY: THE FRAGMENTATION OF CORPORATE GLORY

Glory is both personal and corporate.

At Solomon's temple:

> *"…the Levites stood as one (echad)."*
> *— 2 Chronicles 5:13*

Only then did the glory fall.

Unity creates a landing place for glory.

Division dismantles the corporate dwelling God intends.

A divided people cannot host a unified God.

8. FORM WITHOUT POWER: RELIGION VOID OF PRESENCE

Paul warns of those:

Religion without glory is idolatry dressed in liturgy.

It maintains rituals but lacks revelation.

It performs ceremonies but rejects transformation.

The Pharisees had Scripture—but no presence.

The Sadducees had temple authority—but no glory.

A church, ministry, or believer can maintain activity while the glory silently withdraws.

9. FEAR OF MAN: THE MISPLACED WORSHIP THAT EXPELS GLORY

Fear is a form of worship.

Saul confessed:

> *"I feared the people and obeyed their voice."*
> *— 1 Samuel 15:24*

Fear of man dethrones the fear of the Lord.

Whatever you fear, you exalt.

Whatever you exalt, you enthrone.

Whatever you enthrone governs you.

If people govern your decisions, God does not.

And where God does not rule, His glory does not dwell.

10. NEGLECT OF GOD'S PRESENCE: THE SLOW EXTINCTION OF SACRED FIRE

In Leviticus 6:13, God commands:

"A fire shall always be burning on the altar; it shall never go out."

This fire is symbolic of continual communion.

Neglect—gradual, subtle, unnoticed—allows:

- prayer to fade

- worship to become mechanical

- Scripture to become distant

- repentance to become rare

- holiness to be compromised

Neglect is not rebellion; it is spiritual drift.

But drift is often more dangerous because it is almost invisible.

Where the altar is abandoned, the glory lifts.

THE SEVERITY AND THE MERCY OF GOD: HOW THE GLORY RETURNS

The loss of glory is serious—but it is not final.

The theological pattern for restoration is consistent:

1. Conviction

— God exposes the breach

2. Repentance

— the heart returns to covenant alignment

3. Consecration

— cleansing of sacred space

4. Reestablishment of divine order

— restoring God's rightful place

5. Renewal

— glory returns in greater measure

When the temple was cleansed under Hezekiah, the glory returned.

When Israel repented under Nehemiah and Ezra, the glory returned.

When Christ rose from the dead, glory burst the veil open forever.

The seriousness of losing glory is matched only by the mercy of God to restore it.

Glory leaves legally—but returns relationally, covenantally, mercifully, and powerfully.

CHAPTER SEVEN: ENTERING THE GLORY: THE DIVINE PATTERN OF APPROACHING GOD

The glory of God is not accessed randomly.

It is not stumbled into.

It is not encountered by accident or emotion.

The glory is entered.

And God Himself established the way.

Just as there were patterns for creation, patterns for the tabernacle, patterns for sacrifice, and patterns for priesthood—there is a pattern for glory.

This chapter reveals the ancient pathway, rooted in Hebrew priesthood, mosaic revelation, prophetic symbolism, and fulfilled in Christ, that teaches us how God's people are to enter His glory.

It is not casual.

It is not mechanical.

It is not emotional.

It is holy.

1. THE REVELATION OF GLORY BEGINS WITH GOD'S INITIATIVE

Before man ever approached God, God came down.

- He came down in Eden.

- He came down on Sinai.

- He came down in the Tabernacle.

- He came down in Solomon's Temple.

- He came down in the person of Jesus Christ.

- He came down as the Spirit in Acts 2.

Glory always begins with divine initiative, not human pursuit.

This is why Moses prayed:

> *"...Show me Your glory."*
> *— Exodus 33:18*

He understood that glory is granted, not assumed.

God responded:

"I will make all My goodness pass before you... and I will proclaim the name of the LORD before you."

Revelation:

Glory is God revealing His nature, not God entertaining human desire.

2. THE TABERNACLE PATTERN: GOD'S BLUEPRINT FOR ENTERING HIS GLORY

The Tabernacle was not merely a tent; it was a theological model of the journey into God's glory.

It had three realms:

1. Outer Court — cleansing, sacrifice, justification

2. Holy Place — consecration, illumination, intercession

3. Holy of Holies — the realm of glory

Each realm had purpose and progression.

No one ever jumped into the Most Holy Place—they ascended toward it.

This reveals a divine law:

Glory rests at the end of a process, not at the beginning of one.

You do not enter the Holy of Holies without:

- cleansing at the bronze laver

- dying at the altar

- feeding on the Presence in the Holy Place

- walking in Spirit-illumination

- maintaining intercession at the golden altar

Only then—only then—could the high priest enter the glory.

**3. THE HIGH PRIEST AND THE DAY OF ATONEMENT:

THE MOST SERIOUS APPROACH TO GLORY IN SCRIPTURE**

Leviticus 16 is the heaviest chapter in the Torah on entering God's glory.

Three truths stand out:

A. Only one man—once a year—could enter the glory

Not the priests.

Not the Levites.

Not the congregation.

Only the high priest.

This reveals the exclusivity and sanctity of the glory realm.

B. He could not enter "at all times"

God warns:

"...Tell Aaron... not to come at just any time into the Holy Place... lest he die..."
— Leviticus 16:2

Glory kills what is unclean.

Glory judges what is unprepared.

Glory consumes what is unauthorized.

C. He must enter with blood, incense, and humility

Without:

- blood on the mercy seat

- incense cloud covering him

- linen garments of humility

—he would not survive.

This teaches us:

Glory requires death of self, cleansing by blood, covering by intercession, and abandonment of pride.

The bishop's robes, titles, positions, and crowns meant nothing in the Holy of Holies.

Only humility lived there.

4. THE SMOKE OF INCENSE: A THEOLOGY OF COVERING

The incense cloud was not decoration—it was protection.

The Hebrew word for incense, qetoret, signifies both fragrance and veil.

God commanded:

"...the cloud of incense may cover the mercy seat... lest he die."
— Leviticus 16:13

Theological truth:

****No one stands unveiled before glory.**

Prayer is our covering. Intercession is our shield. **

A prayerless life is an uncovered life.

An uncovered life is a vulnerable life.

A vulnerable life is an exposed life before the holiness of God.

5. THE VEIL: THE BARRIER AND BRIDGE OF GLORY

The veil in Hebrew is parokhet (פ ר כ ת), meaning "curtain of separation."

It symbolized:

- God's holiness

- man's sinfulness

- distance created by rebellion

But when Christ died:

> *"…the veil of the temple was torn in two."*
> — *Matthew 27:51*

This was not symbolic poetry—it was cosmic theology.

The tearing of the veil means:

****The glory is no longer restricted to one man once a year.**

All who are in Christ may now enter. **

Not casually.

Not without reverence.

Not without holiness.

But the way is open.

6. SANCTIFICATION: THE ONLY ACCEPTABLE

STATE FOR ENTERING GLORY

The word sanctify in Hebrew is qadash (ש.ד.ק): set apart, purified, prepared.

In Greek, hagiazō (ἁγιάζω): to make holy, to make suitable for God's presence.

Sanctification is not optional for glory; it is the prerequisite.

Jesus prayed:

> *"Sanctify them by Your truth."*
> *— John 17:17*

Paul writes:

> *"Without holiness no one will see the Lord."*
> *— Hebrews 12:14*

Meaning:

****Holiness is not behavior—it is atmosphere.**

Holiness creates the climate where glory rests.**

The unholy cannot survive the glory realm, not because God is cruel, but because glory is incompatible with sin.

7. BROKENNESS: THE POSTURE THAT INVITES GLORY

The sacrifices of God are:

> *"...a broken and a contrite heart..."*
> *— Psalm 51:17*

Why brokenness?

Because:

- brokenness empties the soul of self

- brokenness dethrones pride

- brokenness removes resistance

- brokenness makes room for God

God dwells with the broken:

"...I dwell... with him who is of a contrite and humble spirit..."
— Isaiah 57:15

Brokenness is the doorway to glory.

A proud man prays, but heaven is silent.

A broken man whispers, and glory descends.

8. THE BLOOD OF JESUS: THE ETERNAL MEANS OF ACCESS

Everything in the Old Covenant pointed to this truth:

"...by His own blood He entered the Most Holy Place once for all..."
— Hebrews 9:12

His blood:

- removed sin

- cleansed the conscience

- satisfied divine justice

- inaugurated a new priesthood

- opened a new and living way

Without the blood, no one enters glory.

With the blood, all who believe may enter—but with reverence.

9. THE SPIRIT OF GOD: OUR GUIDE INTO THE GLORY REALM

Paul teaches:

"...through Him we both have access by one Spirit to the Father."
— Ephesians 2:18

Only the Holy Spirit knows:

- the paths of glory

- the movements of God

- the depths of the divine

- the rhythms of the throne room

Glory is not entered through emotion or effort.

It is entered by the Spirit.

**No Spirit—no access.

More Spirit—more glory. **

10. NEW TESTAMENT GLORY: CHRIST IN US, THE HOPE OF GLORY

Paul reaches the pinnacle of revelation when he writes:

"...Christ in you, the hope of glory."
— Colossians 1:27

The glory Moses saw externally in a cloud,

the believer now carries internally by the Spirit.

This is not metaphor—it is divine reality.

You are a:

- walking tabernacle

- mobile Holy of Holies

- carrier of divine presence

- living ark of covenant

Glory is no longer a place you travel to—it is a Person who dwells in you.

**THE FINAL REVELATION:

GLORY HAS A PATHWAY, AND GOD HAS A PATTERN**

To enter the glory:

1. God must initiate

2. Man must respond

3. The blood must cleanse

4. The Spirit must lead

5. Holiness must surround

6. Humility must cover

7. Brokenness must open the heart

8. Prayer must create atmosphere

9. Sanctification must deepen

10. Christ must be enthroned

The glory is not for the casual seeker.

It is for the consecrated follower.

The pathway to glory is paved with:

- fire

- blood

- tears

- repentance

- reverence

- surrender

- intimacy

- obedience

And the reward is God Himself

CHAPTER EIGHT: MANIFESTATIONS OF GLORY: THE HISTORICAL AND THEOLOGICAL RECORD OF DIVINE REVELATION

The Scriptures are the Holy Spirit's archive of God's dealings with humanity. Within them are recorded the moments when the invisible God made Himself visible, when eternity touched time, and when the weight of His essence rested upon the earth.

These are not isolated miracles.

They are patterns.

They reveal laws of glory.

They unveil conditions under which God reveals Himself and

circumstances under which He withdraws.

In this chapter, we walk through the sacred corridors of Scripture to behold the glory of God as it manifested in various eras—each manifestation unveiling deeper truths about His nature, His holiness, and His covenant.

1. THE GLORY IN EDEN: THE FIRST DWELLING OF GOD WITH MAN

Before sin, Eden was not merely a garden—it was a sanctuary, the prototype of the Temple.

The Hebrew phrase "God walked" (Genesis 3:8) uses the verb hithpael, indicating a habitual, continual movement, not a one-time visitation.

Adam and Eve lived in unbroken fellowship with God's glory.

They were clothed in His light (Psalm 104:2), walking in a realm where:

- heaven touched earth

- God dwelt openly

- creation responded to divine presence

The fall was tragic not primarily because man sinned, but because man lost the glory covering.

Humanity has been seeking restoration ever since.

2. THE GLORY WITH ENOCH: THE GLORY THAT TAKES A MAN

Enoch's testimony was simple yet profound:

"...he walked with God; and he was not, for God took him."

This is more than intimacy.

This is glory absorption.

Enoch walked so deeply into the realm of God that the boundary between earth and heaven dissolved.

Enoch becomes a prototype of the New Covenant believer:

- fully yielded

- fully aligned

- fully saturated with divine presence

- walking in continual communion

The glory is not only something that descends—it is something that carries a man upward.

3. THE GLORY IN THE FLOOD ERA: GOD'S HOLINESS REVEALED IN JUDGMENT

The flood was not merely destruction—it was a cleansing of the defiled sanctuary of earth.

In Hebrew theology, water symbolizes:

- cleansing

- resetting

- new creation

God's judgment was itself a manifestation of His glory because glory is the full revelation of His character—including holiness.

Noah survived because:

- he walked with God

- he found grace (favor, Hebrew ḥēn)

- he obeyed precisely

The ark becomes a type of Christ—the only vessel in which humanity is preserved during judgment.

Where there is obedience, glory preserves.

4. THE GLORY WITH ABRAHAM: THE GOD WHO APPEARS

God appeared to Abraham multiple times (Genesis 12, 15, 17, 18).

The Hebrew verb ra'ah (הָאָרְ) means to reveal, to cause to see.

The covenant with Abraham was sealed in glory, not theology.

Most significantly, Genesis 15 records a theophany where:

- a smoking furnace

- and a burning lamp
  —passed between animal pieces

These images represent God's glory passing between the covenant sacrifice.

Abraham was asleep—because the covenant depended entirely on God.

Glory reveals:

Everything begins with God, not man.

5. THE GLORY WITH MOSES: THE MOUNTAIN OF FIRE

Mount Sinai becomes the most dramatic revelation of glory in the Old Testament.

The glory appeared as:

- fire

- smoke

- earthquake

- trumpet blast

- thick darkness

- visible flame

"...the mountain burned with fire to the midst of heaven..."
— Deuteronomy 4:11

These were not theatrics but manifestations of God's holiness.

And yet the greatest revelation was not the fire—but the voice.

God's voice is the ultimate expression of His glory.

Israel saw the fire—but only Moses ascended into it.

This reveals:

****Those who fear God watch His glory.**

Those who love God climb into His glory. **

6. THE GLORY IN THE TABERNACLE: GOD DWELLING AMONG HIS PEOPLE

Exodus 40 describes the moment the tabernacle was finished:

"...the glory of the LORD filled the tabernacle."
— Exodus 40:34

Three theological truths emerge:

A. God dwells where His pattern is followed

Moses built exactly as God commanded.

Glory does not rest on human creativity—only on divine order.

B. The glory rested on the mercy seat

The mercy seat was the place of:

- blood atonement

- intercession

- covenant faithfulness

Blood and glory cannot be separated.

C. The glory guided Israel

The cloud by day, fire by night.

Glory is both dwelling and direction.

7. THE GLORY IN SOLOMON'S TEMPLE: THE HEAVIEST GLORY EVER RECORDED

When Solomon dedicated the temple, something extraordinary happened:

> *"...the priests could not stand to minister..."*
> *— 2 Chronicles 5:14*

This was not emotional worship.

This was weight—the literal heaviness of God's presence.

Key truths:

Unity preceded glory

The musicians were "as one" (echad).

Sacrifice preceded glory

22,000 oxen and 120,000 sheep were offered.

Holiness preceded glory

The ark, the priests, the singers—all sanctified.

Glory is not random; it comes where the price has been paid.

8. THE GLORY IN THE PROPHETS: EZEKIEL'S VISIONS

Ezekiel's visions of the glory are the most detailed in Scripture:

- wheels within wheels

- living creatures

- the sapphire throne

- the fiery expanse

- the rainbow of emerald radiance

- the sound of many waters

This is the architecture of glory—the throne room of God.

But Ezekiel also saw:

the glory departing the temple

This is the most sobering revelation of all.

Sin did not remove God suddenly—it escorted Him out step by step.

Israel continued worshiping

continued sacrificing

continued gathering

—but the glory was gone.

This is the danger of religion without presence.

9. THE GLORY IN CHRIST: THE WORD MADE VISIBLE

John writes:

> *"…we beheld His glory…"*
> *— John 1:14*

Jesus was the embodied glory—the exact expression (charaktēr) of God's nature.

Consider His manifestations of glory:

- Transfiguration: face shining like the sun

- Miracles: glory through compassion

- Resurrection: glory defeating death

- Ascension: glory returning to the Father

Christ is not a reflection of glory—

He is the source of glory.

10. THE GLORY IN THE CHURCH: THE SPIRIT CONSUMES THE TEMPLE

Acts 2 is the New Covenant Sinai.

The same manifestations appear:

- fire

- wind

- sound

- divine speech

Except this time, the fire divided and rested on each believer.

No longer one man once a year.

No longer one place once a generation.

The glory became a shared inheritance.

Believers became:

- mobile sanctuaries

- walking temples

- carriers of the Shekinah

- living arks of the covenant

Pentecost was not a revival.

It was a relocation of glory—from a building to a people.

11. THE GLORY IN THE NEW CREATION: THE CITY OF GLORY

Revelation describes a future where:

- the city has no temple

- the Lamb is its light

- the nations walk in His glory

- the throne radiates emerald fire

- the redeemed shine like the sun

This is the destiny of the believer:

> *"...to be glorified together with Him."*
> *— Romans 8:17*

Glory is not merely an experience.

It is our final transformation.

THE FINAL REVELATION OF THIS CHAPTER

Every manifestation of glory in Scripture reveals one truth:

God desires to dwell with man.

From Eden to the New Jerusalem, the heartbeat of God is the same:

> *"...I will dwell among them..."*
> *— Leviticus 26:12*

Glory is not a feeling.

It is God Himself.

And He is calling His people back into the realm where:

- sin dies

- flesh bows

- holiness is restored

- revelation flows

- intimacy deepens

- transformation begins

- heaven touches earth

The glory of God is both our origin and our destiny.

It is where humanity began—and where the redeemed will end.

**CHAPTER NINE:
THE RESTORATION OF
GLORY:
THE DIVINE PATHWAY
BACK INTO GOD'S
MANIFEST PRESENCE**

If Chapter Six revealed the causes of glory loss, and Chapters Seven and Eight unveiled how glory is approached and revealed, then the natural burden of the Spirit is now to show how the glory returns when it has been lifted.

For every departure of the glory in Scripture, God also revealed a path of return.

This path is not emotionalism, not desperation, not ritual, not loud worship—

it is a covenant restoration process, rooted in:

- repentance

- cleansing

- reconstruction

- re-consecration

- re-enthronement of God

- holiness

- and renewed covenant alignment

This chapter explores the theology of glory restoration, proven repeatedly through Scripture.

1. THE FIRST PRINCIPLE: GOD DESIRES TO RESTORE HIS GLORY MORE THAN MAN DESIRES TO SEEK IT

When Israel sinned, God withdrew—but never abandoned.

In Ezekiel, right after the glory departs (chapters 8–10), God gives a promise:

"...I will give them one heart... a new spirit... and remove the heart of stone..."
— Ezekiel 11:19

Meaning:

God Himself initiates every restoration of glory.

Restoration begins in God's heart, not man's desperation.

Revival is not man reaching up—

it is God reaching down.

2. THE GLORY CANNOT RETURN UNTIL THE ALTAR IS REPAIRED

When Elijah confronted Israel on Mount Carmel, Israel had:

- altars

- prophets

- sacrifices

- religious gatherings

…but no glory.

The first thing God required.

"…Elijah repaired the altar of the LORD that was broken down."
— 1 Kings 18:30

The altar symbolizes:

- broken worship

- forsaken devotion

- abandoned prayer

- lost sacrifice

- misplaced priorities

This is why revival does not begin with music or meetings—

it begins with altar repair.

Only after the altar was restored did fire (glory) fall.

3. THE GLORY RETURNS WHERE THERE IS TRUE

REPENTANCE (NOT APOLOGY)

Repentance in Hebrew is teshuvah—literally "to return, to come back to the point of origin."

Repentance is not:

* tears

* emotions

* regret

It is a return to God's order, God's throne, God's holiness, God's government.

The New Testament word metanoia means a complete renewal of mind and direction.

Every restoration in Scripture begins with repentance:

* Nineveh

* Hezekiah's reforms

* Josiah's revival

* The return from Babylon

* John the Baptist preparing the way

* Pentecost

Repentance cleanses the temple of the heart so glory may return.

4. THE GLORY RETURNS WHERE THERE IS CLEANSING OF SACRED SPACE

Before God returned to the temple in the days of Hezekiah:

* the priests removed filth

- the Levites sanctified themselves

- the temple was purged

- unclean objects were taken out

Only then:

> *"...the glory of the LORD appeared..."*
> *— 2 Chronicles 7*

This is divine order:

**Cleansing precedes glory.

Purging precedes presence.

Holiness precedes habitation.**

God will not dwell where pollution remains unchallenged.

5. THE GLORY RETURNS WHERE THE WORD OF GOD IS RESTORED

Every revival in Scripture includes a restoration of the Word:

- Ezra stood and read the Law—revival broke out

- Josiah rediscovered the Book of the Law—revival erupted

- Samuel restored prophetic integrity—glory returned

- Jesus preached repentance—kingdom glory manifested

- Acts 2 believers devoted themselves to the apostles' doctrine—glory multiplied

Where the Word is absent, the glory is silent.

Where the Word is honored, glory speaks again.

6. THE GLORY RETURNS WHERE GOD IS RE-ENTHRONED

In the Old Covenant, the glory rested on the mercy seat, God's throne on earth.

Wherever God's throne is dishonored:

- idolatry arises

- self reigns

- flesh dominates

- corruption grows

To restore the glory, God must be re-enthroned.

This requires:

- dethroning idols

- dismantling self-will

- renouncing pride

- yielding authority

- restoring God's supremacy

Glory descends only where God is King, not consultant.

7. THE GLORY RETURNS WHERE WORSHIP IS PURE AND SACRIFICE IS ACCEPTABLE

David restored the ark through:

- sanctified worship

- consecrated singers

- sacrifices offered in order

- obedience to priestly instruction

When worship was corrected, the glory returned.

This shows:

**Worship is not for entertainment.

Worship is priestly.

Worship is warfare.

Worship is glory alignment. **

God only inhabits the worship that is offered from consecrated hearts.

8. THE GLORY RETURNS THROUGH A RENEWED PRIESTHOOD

Where priests are corrupt, glory departs.

Where priests are restored, glory returns.

In the New Covenant, YOU are the priest.

Your priesthood must be:

- purified

- consecrated

- disciplined

- in order

- clothed in righteousness

- faithful in intercession

The glory does not come on casual priests—

only consecrated ones.

9. THE GLORY RETURNS THROUGH THE BLOOD OF JESUS APPLIED AFRESH

Hebrews reveals the ultimate truth:

"...having boldness to enter the Holiest by the blood..."
— Hebrews 10:19

Restoration of glory requires:

- renewed faith in the blood

- renewed gratitude for the cross

- renewed cleansing of conscience

- renewed dependence on grace

The blood opens the way for glory every time.

10. THE GLORY RETURNS THROUGH THE HOLY SPIRIT'S FRESH OUTPOURING

The glory does not come by:

- programs

- talent

- charisma

- human wisdom

- building structures

- emotional hype

It comes by Spirit outpouring.

Every restoration of glory in Scripture involved the Spirit:

- Judges 3–16 (cycles of deliverance)

- David's anointing

- Ezekiel's visions

- Joel's prophecy

- Acts 2

- Acts 10

- Acts 19

The Spirit brings the glory, reveals the glory, and sustains the glory.

THE FINAL REVELATION OF THIS CHAPTER

The return of the glory is not random.

It follows divine laws:

- Repentance restores alignment

- Holiness restores atmosphere

- Worship restores God's throne

- The Word restores foundation

- The Spirit restores life

- The blood restores access

- Cleansing restores purity

- Consecration restores identity

These are the pillars upon which glory rests.

God desires to restore His glory to His people.

But He will not restore it to an unprepared people.

****The glory returns where God is honored.**

The glory dwells where God is obeyed.

The glory remains where God is enthroned. **

CHAPTER TEN: SUSTAINING THE GLORY: THE SPIRITUAL LAWS THAT KEEP THE PRESENCE OF GOD AMONG HIS PEOPLE

The glory of God is a gift, but sustaining the glory is a responsibility.

Throughout Scripture, we see a pattern:

- The glory comes.

- The glory rests.

- The glory tests.

- The glory stays or departs based on how it is treated.

Where glory is valued, it increases.

Where glory is neglected, it diminishes.

Where glory is dishonored, it departs.

This chapter explores the spiritual disciplines, priestly practices, and covenantal principles required to maintain the glory of God once it has been restored.

1. THE FIRST PRINCIPLE: THE GLORY REMAINS WHERE GOD REMAINS FIRST

God does not rest where He is not central.

Glory abides only where God is enthroned.

Jesus taught:

> *"Seek first the kingdom of God..."*
> *— Matthew 6:33*

First — prōton (πρῶτον): priority, order, supremacy.

This means:

- First in affection

- First in decision making

- First in time

- First in obedience

- First in honor

Where God is first, glory remains.

Where God becomes an accessory, glory lifts.

2. MAINTAINING THE ALTAR OF FIRE:

CONTINUAL SACRIFICE

God commanded Israel:

"The fire on the altar shall never go out."
— Leviticus 6:13

This was not about natural flame —

it was a prophetic picture of the human heart.

To maintain glory, the altar of your life must remain:

- burning

- active

- consecrated

- sacrificial

- watchful

When the altar dies, the glory lifts.

When the altar burns, glory rests.

This requires:

- daily prayer

- continual communion

- consistent fasting

- disciplined consecration

- daily surrender

Glory is not maintained through occasional devotion but continual fire.

3. HOLINESS AS A LIFESTYLE, NOT AN EVENT

Holiness in Hebrew is qadosh (שׁ.דוֹ.ק):

separated, distinct, set apart, pure.

In Greek, hagios:

 belonging to God.

Holiness is not moral perfection.

It is alignment with God's nature.

Holiness sustains glory because:

- glory rests on purity

- glory reveals God's nature

- glory exposes darkness

- glory amplifies righteousness

The moment holiness is compromised; glory becomes grieved.

This is why the early church experienced continual glory:

> *"...they continued steadfastly..."*
> *— Acts 2:42*

Holiness was their rhythm, not their emergency.

4. OBEDIENCE — THE GLORY KEEPER

It is impossible to sustain glory with partial obedience.

Jesus said:

> *"If you love Me, keep My commandments."*
> *— John 14:15*

Obedience is the oxygen of glory.

Obedience sustains:

- intimacy

- purity

- authority

- revelation

- spiritual sensitivity

Disobedience suffocates the glory, slowly and silently.

Where obedience is immediate, the glory remains strong.

5. GUARDING THE GATES — WATCHFULNESS AND DISCERNMENT

In the spirit realm, glory is easily contaminated by what is allowed through the gates:

- eye gate

- ear gate

- mouth gate

- heart gate

Proverbs teaches:

> *"Guard your heart with all diligence..."*
> *— Proverbs 4:23*

Why?

Because the glory resides in the heart, and whatever enters the heart either strengthens or pollutes it.

To maintain the glory, the believer must guard against:

- careless entertainment

- corrupt speech

- ungodly relationships

- spiritual apathy

- demonic infiltration

- compromise in any form

Watchfulness keeps the inner sanctuary pure.

6. LIVING IN THE FEAR OF THE LORD

The fear of the LORD is the environment where the glory thrives.

Isaiah declares:

> *"The fear of the LORD is His treasure."*
> *— Isaiah 33:6*

Fear of the Lord means:

- reverence

- awe

- trembling

- submission

- hatred of sin

- deep respect for holy things

Where the fear of the Lord is absent, glory becomes optional.

Where the fear of the Lord is cultivated, glory becomes continual.

7. STAYING LOW: HUMILITY AS THE RESTING PLACE OF GLORY

God does not rest on the powerful.

He rests on the humble.

> *"...to this one I will look:*
> *to him who is humble and contrite in spirit..."*
> *— Isaiah 66:2*

Humility sustains glory because:

- it removes pride (the original glory thief)

- it keeps self off the throne

- it allows God to increase

- it keeps the heart teachable

- it protects against spiritual arrogance

The lower a person goes, the heavier the glory becomes.

8. THE WORD OF GOD — THE FOUNDATION THAT KEEPS GLORY FROM DRIFTING

Glory does not rest on emotion—

it rests on truth.

Jesus said:

> *"Sanctify them by Your truth; Your Word is truth."*
> *— John 17:17*

To sustain glory:

- the Word must saturate the mind

- Scripture must govern decisions

- truth must confront compromise

- doctrine must remain pure

- meditation must be continual

The Word is the anchor that prevents glory from drifting.

Where the Word is honored, the glory remains stable.

9. SUBMISSION TO THE HOLY SPIRIT — THE KEEPER OF GLORY

The glory is not sustained through human effort.

It is sustained through yielding to the Holy Spirit —

the Spirit of glory (1 Peter 4:14).

To maintain glory:

- obey His impulses

- yield to His corrections

- follow His guidance

- remain sensitive to His whispers

- avoid grieving or quenching Him

Where the Spirit is honored, the glory remains vibrant.

10. COMMUNITY AND UNITY — GLORY IS A CORPORATE REALITY

Although glory can fill an individual,

it thrives in a corporate environment of unity.

In Acts 4:

"...they lifted their voice with one accord...

and the place was shaken..."

Unity creates a dwelling place for God.

Division repels glory.

Unity multiplies it.

This is why Satan attacks relationships —

because he fears corporate glory.

11. CONSISTENT CONSECRATION — THE GLORY MUST BE PROTECTED

Consecration is not a moment; it is a lifestyle.

To maintain glory, a believer must:

- continually separate from worldliness

- refuse carnal entanglements

- purge spiritual contamination

- maintain a posture of surrender

- keep the heart pure and uncluttered

Consecration is the fence around the glory.

12. FRESH OIL — GLORY THRIVES ON RENEWAL

David prayed:

"I shall be anointed with fresh oil."
— Psalm 92:10

Glory must be renewed, refreshed, replenished.

This means:

- fresh encounters

- fresh revelations

- fresh worship

- fresh surrender

- fresh hunger for God

Stagnation kills glory.

Fresh oil sustains it.

THE FINAL REVELATION OF THIS CHAPTER

Receiving the glory is a miracle.

But maintaining it is a priesthood.

Glory remains where:

- altars burn

- holiness lives

- humility reigns

- obedience flows

- truth governs

- the Spirit leads

- consecration is constant

- unity is valued

- the fear of the Lord is cultivated

- God is enthroned above all

The glory of God is not a moment —

it is a realm.

And living in that realm requires deliberate, sacred, continual stewardship.

Where God is honored, glory remains.

Where God is obeyed, glory rests.

Where God is loved, glory dwells.

**CHAPTER ELEVEN:
THE TRANSFORMATION
OF GLORY:
HOW THE PRESENCE OF
GOD CHANGES A PERSON
FROM THE INSIDE OUT**

The glory of God is not passive.

It does not come to admire; it comes to transform.

Whenever glory appears in Scripture, something changes:

- Moses' face begins to shine

- Isaiah is undone and recommissioned

- Ezekiel collapses under divine weight

- The disciples fall on their faces

- Paul is blinded and reborn

- John becomes a man of revelation

- The early church is empowered with boldness

Glory never leaves a person as it found them.

It restructures.

It sanctifies.

It illuminates.

It purifies.

It transforms.

This chapter unveils the spiritual mechanics, covenant theology, and divine process by which the glory of God reshapes a human being into the image of Christ.

1. THE FIRST WORK OF GLORY: EXPOSURE AND REVELATION OF SELF

Before glory transforms, it reveals.

Isaiah encountered God's glory and cried:

"Woe is me! I am undone…"
— Isaiah 6:5

Undone in Hebrew (dāmāh, הִמְָדָ) means:

- ruined

- dismantled

- dissolved

- taken apart

This is the first work of glory —

the dismantling of pride, ego, flesh, and illusion.

Glory exposes:

- hidden motives

- secret sins

- heart postures

- spiritual blindness

- areas of compromise

But exposure is not condemnation—

it is preparation for transformation.

2. GLORY PURIFIES — THE THEOLOGY OF HOLY FIRE

When Isaiah saw the glory, a seraph touched his lips with a burning coal:

> *"...your iniquity is taken away..."*
> *— Isaiah 6:7*

Glory does not only reveal sin —

it burns it out.

In Scripture, fire is not judgment alone but purification:

- Moses' bush burned but was not consumed

- The altar burned continually

- Elijah called fire to restore covenant

- John the Baptist spoke of Holy Spirit fire

- Tongues of fire fell at Pentecost

Fire burns away:

- uncleanness

- rebellion

- wrong desires

- spiritual contamination

- demonic influences

Where glory rests, sanctification accelerates.

3. GLORY REVEALS GOD — THE KNOWLEDGE OF THE HOLY

Moses prayed:

> *"Show me Your glory."*
> *— Exodus 33:18*

God answered:

> *"I will make all My goodness pass before you,*
>
> *and I will proclaim the name of the LORD…"*
> *— Exodus 33:19*

Thus, glory revealed:

- God's name

- God's character

- God's nature

- God's ways

- God's heart

- God's covenant faithfulness

Glory is the classroom of God's nature.

Where glory rests, revelation increases.

4. GLORY TRANSFORMS THE SOUL — FROM GLORY TO GLORY

Paul gives the deepest revelation:

> *"...we are transformed into the same image*
>
> *from glory to glory..."*
> *— 2 Corinthians 3:18*

The Greek word for transformed is metamorphoō—

the same word used for Jesus' transfiguration.

This means:

Glory does not improve you — it changes you.

Not externally — but internally.

Not temporarily — but continually. **

Glory rewires:

- desires

- thinking

- emotional patterns

- responses

- affections

- identity

- spiritual perception

The more glory you behold…

the more like Him you become.

5. GLORY RESTORES LOST IDENTITY

Before the fall, Adam carried glory.

He lost identity when he lost glory.

When glory returns to a person:

- identity is healed

- purpose becomes clear

- spiritual authority is restored

- divine assignment awakens

- confidence in God increases

This is why Satan fears the glory —

because glory restores what he stole.

6. GLORY BRINGS DIVINE ORDER INTO THE CHAOS OF THE SOUL

In Genesis 1, the first manifestation of God was glory moving upon chaos.

Before creation formed, the Spirit hovered.

Before light appeared, glory was present.

This reveals a spiritual law:

Where glory comes, chaos must yield.

In the believer:

- emotional storms calm

- mental confusion clears

- inner conflict dissolves

- anxiety breaks

- depression lifts

- double-mindedness stabilizes

- disorder submits to divine order

Glory is the government of God operating inside the human heart.

7. GLORY EMPOWERS FOR SERVICE — THE COMMISSION OF GOD

Every time glory appears, a divine assignment follows:

- Moses is commissioned to deliver Israel

- Isaiah is commissioned to prophesy

- Ezekiel is commissioned to warn

- Jeremiah receives divine speech

- Paul receives apostolic purpose

No one touched by glory lives a life of aimlessness.

Glory does not only transform —

it commissions.

It releases:

- spiritual authority

- boldness

- courage

- prophetic clarity

- apostolic endurance

- supernatural empowerment

Glory creates servants who carry God's burden.

8. GLORY MAKES THE BELIEVER A CONDUIT OF GOD'S POWER

The early church moved in miracles because they lived in glory.

Acts 4:

> *"...they prayed; the place was shaken..."*

Acts 5:

> *"...great power and great grace was upon them all..."*

Glory enables:

- healing

- deliverance

- spiritual authority

- bold preaching

- supernatural discernment

- prophetic inspiration

The believer becomes:

- a temple of presence

- a carrier of fire

- a vessel of power

- a representation of Christ

- a walking ark of covenant

Glory makes you a gateway through which heaven touches earth.

9. GLORY MAKES YOU INTO GOD'S HABITATION

Paul reveals the ultimate mystery:

> *"...Christ in you, the hope of glory."*
> *— Colossians 1:27*

Glory is not just something you encounter —

it is Someone who dwells in you.

The Spirit makes the believer:

- a living sanctuary

- a dwelling place of God

- a throne room of grace

- a carrier of divine presence

This is why transformation is inevitable —

because glory lives inside the believer.

10. GLORY MAKES YOU LIKE CHRIST — THE FINAL GOAL

Paul declares:

> *"...when He appears, we shall be like Him..."*
> — *1 John 3:2*

This is the end of transformation —

the believer reflecting the image of the Son.

Glory transforms the believer into:

- the character of Christ

- the purity of Christ

- the mind of Christ

- the love of Christ

- the authority of Christ

- the humility of Christ

- the obedience of Christ

Glory restores the lost image.

It produces sons and daughters who reflect the Father.

THE FINAL REVELATION OF THIS CHAPTER

Glory is not merely an experience.

It is a force.

A fire.

A sanctifying presence.

A transforming power that:

- exposes

- purifies

- renews

- reshapes

- recommissions

- empowers

- indwells

- transfigures

The purpose of glory is not excitement —

it is transformation into the likeness of Christ.

The more we behold Him,

the more we become like Him.

This is the ultimate outcome of dwelling in the glory:

Christ formed in us, and us conformed to Christ.

**CHAPTER TWELVE:
THE GLORY AS WARFARE:
HOW THE MANIFEST
PRESENCE OF GOD
DESTROYS DARKNESS,
SHIFTS ATMOSPHERES,
AND ESTABLISHES
DOMINION**

The glory of God does not simply transform the believer inwardly—

it also confronts the enemy outwardly.

Where glory rests, darkness trembles.

Where glory manifests, strongholds collapse.

Where glory increases, Satan's influence is broken.

This chapter reveals the spiritual warfare dimension of glory, rooted in Scripture, Scripture, and displayed through the history of redemption.

The believer is not only called to carry glory—

but to advance it.

1. GLORY IS THE MANIFESTATION OF GOD'S GOVERNMENT

In Scripture, the glory is never merely a "feeling."

It is the visible expression of God's throne.

Where God's throne is present, His government is active.

David writes:

> *"The LORD reigns… He is clothed with majesty."*
> *— Psalm 93:1*

Majesty and glory are governmental terms.

When glory appears:

- God rules

- angels move

- demons scatter

- darkness flees

- the kingdom advances

Glory is not passive — it is government in motion.

Where glory rests, warfare shifts instantly.

2. GLORY TERRIFIES THE KINGDOM OF DARKNESS

James writes:

> *"...the demons believe — and tremble!"*
> *— James 2:19*

Why?

Because they have seen His glory.

Demons fear:

- the presence

- the power

- the holiness

- the authority

- the consuming fire

- the righteousness of God

When glory manifests, demons cannot remain comfortable.

They must:

- flee

- scream

- manifest

- surrender territory

- release captives

- break their hold

Glory enforces the victory already won by Christ.

3. GLORY AS FIRE — GOD'S WEAPON OF WAR

Throughout Scripture, glory appears as fire:

- the fiery bush

- the fiery pillar

- the fiery mountain

- the fiery throne

- the fiery angels

- the fiery chariots

- the tongues of fire at Pentecost

Fire represents three realities:

1. Purification

2. Judgment

3. Warfare

God declares:

> *"…I will be a wall of fire around her…"*
> — *Zechariah 2:5*

God's glory becomes a protective barrier,

a burning shield,

a flaming fortress.

Glory is not only warmth — it is weaponry.

4. THE GLORY CLOUD AS A WEAPON AGAINST

THE ENEMY

During the Exodus, the glory cloud played a military role.

When Israel was trapped:

> *"...the Angel of God... moved and went behind them..."*
> *— Exodus 14:19*

The cloud shifted from guidance to warfare.

To Israel, the cloud brought:

- illumination

- protection

- direction

To Egypt, the same cloud brought:

- confusion

- darkness

- blindness

This teaches a profound truth:

The glory is light to God's people and darkness to His enemies.

It empowers the righteous while disorienting the wicked.

5. GLORY SHIFTS ATMOSPHERES AND DRIVES OUT DARKNESS

Darkness cannot coexist with light.

Darkness is not equal to light.

It is the absence of light.

When glory manifests:

- demonic atmospheres break

- oppression lifts

- depression loosens

- deception is exposed

- heaviness disappears

- the environment changes instantly

This is why the early church prayed:

"...stretch out Your hand... and signs and wonders be done..."
— Acts 4:30

And the place shook.

Glory creates shockwaves in the spiritual realm.

6. GLORY PARALYZES THE ENEMY'S STRATEGY

When the Philistines captured the ark, they thought they had defeated Israel.

But when they placed the ark in Dagon's temple:

- Dagon fell

- Dagon shattered

- tumors broke out

- panic filled the region

The ark represented God's glory.

This story reveals:

Where glory resides, idols fall.

Where glory enters, powers are broken.

Where glory stands, the enemy cannot remain standing. **

The glory did more in one night than armies could have done in a year.

One moment of glory >>> any strategy of man.

7. THE GLORY REALM AND ANGELIC ACTIVITY

Angels operate in the realm of glory.

This is why angels appeared:

- in the glory cloud

- around the throne

- in visions of fire

- at the resurrection

- at the ascension

- at the glory birth of Christ

Where glory is present:

- angels strengthen

- angels protect

- angels execute judgment

- angels deliver messages

- angels war against demonic powers

The believer who dwells in glory becomes aligned with angelic enforcement of God's will.

8. GLORY AS THE SOURCE OF SPIRITUAL AUTHORITY

Authority does not come from:

* shouting

* volume

* personality

* charisma

* memorized prayers

Authority comes from presence.

When the sons of Sceva tried to cast out demons, they had words but no glory.

The demon responded:

> *"Jesus I know, Paul I know, but who are you?"*
> *—Acts 19:15*

Paul was known in the spirit realm because he carried glory-backed authority.

Authority flows from:

* abiding

* intimacy

* purity

* obedience

- revelation

- glory

Without glory, authority is empty.

With glory, a whisper carries more weight than a shout.

9. GLORY ENFORCES THE FINISHED WORK OF CHRIST

Jesus triumphed over Satan through:

- His blood

- His death

- His resurrection

- His ascension

- His enthronement

But the enforcement of that victory occurs where glory manifests.

Glory is the administration of Christ's victory.

This is why Paul calls it:

> *"...the Spirit of glory and of God..."*
> *— 1 Peter 4:14*

The Spirit of glory makes the victory of Christ visible, experiential, and undeniable.

10. GLORY MANIFESTS THE KINGDOM — THE INVASION OF GOD

Jesus declared:

> *"...if I cast out demons by the Spirit of God,*

Where the kingdom comes, glory comes.

Where glory comes, the kingdom confronts darkness.

The kingdom is not a theory —

it is invasion.

And glory is the air of that kingdom.

This is why Jesus said:

"...the kingdom of God is within you."
— Luke 17:21

Meaning:

you carry the atmosphere that destroys the works of the devil.

THE FINAL REVELATION OF THIS CHAPTER

Glory is not only:

- presence

- intimacy

- transformation

Glory is also:

- warfare

- dominion

- authority

- enforcement of Christ's victory

- the dismantling of darkness

This is why Satan fears the glory more than anything else:

- He cannot infiltrate it

- He cannot corrupt it

- He cannot resist it

- He cannot stand before it

- He cannot endure it

- He cannot defeat it

When a believer walks in sustained glory:

- demons recognize them

- atmospheres shift around them

- prophetic clarity sharpens

- spiritual authority increases

- the kingdom advances wherever they go

To carry the glory is to carry the invasion of heaven into the realm of earth.

**CHAPTER THIRTEEN:
THE GLORY AND
INTIMACY:
THE HOLY COMMUNION
BETWEEN GOD AND THE
SOUL**

The highest purpose of glory is not miracles.

Not revelation.

Not transformation.

Not warfare.

Not power.

The highest purpose of glory is fellowship.

From Eden to Revelation, the intention of God has always been:

"...that I may dwell among them..."
— Exodus 25:8

And again:

"...the tabernacle of God is with men..."
— Revelation 21:3

Glory is not God visiting man —

it is God dwelling with man.

This chapter opens the inner chamber of divine intimacy,

the holy romance between the Creator and the redeemed,

the communion that glory makes possible.

1. INTIMACY BEGINS WHERE THE GLORY DWELLS

In the Old Covenant, intimacy with God was limited:

- one man (the high priest)

- once a year

- behind a veil

- with blood offered

But when Christ died, the veil tore (Matthew 27:51),

and the Holy of Holies — the realm of pure glory —

was opened to every believer.

This change in covenant reveals a divine truth:

**Glory is no longer restricted to the priesthood —

glory produces intimacy for every son and daughter. **

Intimacy is possible because glory is accessible.

2. GLORY IS THE REALM OF FACE-TO-FACE FELLOWSHIP

Moses' relationship with God was defined by one phrase:

"...the LORD spoke to Moses face to face..."
— Exodus 33:11

The Hebrew word for face is panim (פ.נ.ים),

which also means presence.

In Scripture, "face" and "glory" are inseparable.

To seek His face is to seek His glory.

To experience His glory is to encounter His face.

Glory is not a cloud—

it is a Person.

It is God revealing Himself.

3. GLORY CREATES THE ATMOSPHERE OF INTIMACY

In Eden, man walked with God because he lived in glory.

In Revelation, man walks with God because he is restored to glory.

In between those two points is the entire storyline of Scripture:

- fall from glory

- longing for glory

- revelation of glory

- restoration of glory

- dwelling in glory forever

Intimacy is the center of this story.

The deeper the glory, the deeper the intimacy.

The deeper the intimacy, the deeper the glory.

This cycle is eternal.

4. GLORY REVEALS THE HEART OF GOD TO MAN

Paul writes:

"...God, who commanded the light to shine out of darkness,

has shone in our hearts to give the light of the knowledge of His glory..."
— 2 Corinthians 4:6

Glory reveals:

- God's emotions

- God's desires

- God's compassion

- God's holiness

- God's voice

- God's heart posture toward His children

Intimacy is not possible without revelation.

Revelation is not possible without glory.

5. INTIMACY IN GLORY REQUIRES VULNERABILITY

To enter glory, the soul must become open.

The flesh cannot hide in glory.

Pretense cannot survive in glory.

Masks dissolve in glory.

Emotional walls melt in glory.

This is why the psalmist prayed:

> *"Search me, O God...*
> *try my heart..."*
> *— Psalm 139:23–24*

Only the heart that allows God to search it

can also allow God to fill it.

Vulnerability is the pathway to intimacy

and the doorway to glory.

6. THE FIRE OF GLORY IS THE FIRE OF LOVE

Song of Solomon describes divine love:

> *"... its flames are flames of fire,*
> *a most vehement flame."*
> *— Song of Solomon 8:6*

This is the same fire that descended upon Sinai,

the same fire that appeared on the altar,

the same fire that rested on the apostles.

The fire of glory is the fire of divine love.

The Holy Spirit is both:

- Spirit of Glory

- Spirit of Love

(1 Peter 4:14; Romans 5:5)

This fire burns away barriers between God and man

and draws them into union.

7. INTIMACY PRODUCES KNOWING — NOT INFORMATION BUT UNION

Jesus said:

> *"…this is eternal life: that they may KNOW You…"*
> *— John 17:3*

The Greek word for know is ginōskō —

relational knowing, experiential knowing, covenant knowing.

This is the kind of knowing that Adam had with Eve.

It produces fruitfulness.

Intimacy with God produces:

- revelation

- fruit of the Spirit

- sensitivity to His voice

- spiritual maturity

- wisdom

- supernatural discernment

Glory transforms knowing God from a concept

into a shared life.

8. GLORY AND WORSHIP — THE LANGUAGE OF INTIMACY

True worship is not music —

it is union.

Worship is where:

- hearts melt

- spirits ascend

- souls yield

- God reveals

- intimacy deepens

The Father seeks worshipers

not for songs

but for relationship.

Jesus said:

"...true worshipers will worship the Father in spirit and truth..."
— John 4:23

This worship happens in glory.

Worship is intimacy expressed.

Glory is intimacy experienced.

9. GLORY AND PRAYER — THE DIALOGUE OF LOVE

Prayer in the glory realm is no longer request-based.

It becomes:

- communion

- sharing of hearts

- divine impressions

- resting in presence

- receiving revelation

- interceding with God's heartbeat

In glory, prayer moves from asking to knowing,

from striving to flowing,

from labor to union.

This is why Paul said:

> *"...the Spirit Himself makes intercession for us..."*
> *— Romans 8:26*

In glory, God prays through you.

**10. THE HIGHEST REALITY OF GLORY:

BECOMING ONE WITH GOD**

Jesus prayed the most intimate prayer ever recorded:

> *"...that they may be ONE as We are ONE..."*
> *— John 17:22*

This is the purpose of glory:

> *"...the GLORY which You gave Me*
> *I have given them,*
> *that they may be one..."*
> *— John 17:22*

Glory makes union possible.

Not equality — union.

Not independence — communion.

Glory enables:

* the mind of Christ

* the heart of the Father

* the leading of the Spirit

* the character of holiness

The believer becomes a participant

in the divine nature (2 Peter 1:4).

Not by effort —

by glory.

THE FINAL REVELATION OF THIS CHAPTER

The greatest gift God gives is not:

* power

* ministry

- revelation

- miracles

- influence

- experiences

The greatest gift God gives is Himself.

Glory is the realm where God and the believer

meet heart to heart,

spirit to spirit,

face to face.

The ultimate purpose of glory is intimacy.

The ultimate result of intimacy is transformation.

The ultimate fruit of transformation is union.

Glory leads to intimacy.

Intimacy leads to union.

Union leads to likeness.

Likeness leads to glory again.

It is a divine cycle,

unending and eternal.

CHAPTER FOURTEEN: THE GLORY AND THE VOICE OF GOD: HEARING, DISCERNING, AND OBEYING THE SPEAKING PRESENCE

The glory of God is not silent.

It is the speaking presence of the Almighty.

Every manifestation of glory in Scripture contains a voice:

- In Eden, God walked and spoke with Adam.

- On Sinai, glory descended and God thundered His voice.

- In the tabernacle, the voice came from between the cherubim.

- In the Temple, the glory filled the house, and God spoke through the priests and prophets.

- At the baptism of Jesus, the heavens opened and the Father spoke.

- At the Transfiguration, glory overshadowed them and a voice declared the Son's identity.

- In Acts 2, glory came as fire and the Spirit gave utterance.

- In Revelation, John saw glory and heard a voice like many waters.

Where glory dwells, God speaks.

Where God speaks, glory is present.

This chapter reveals the theology, mechanics, and atmosphere of the divine voice.

1. THE FIRST TRUTH: THE VOICE OF GOD FLOWS OUT OF GLORY, NOT OUT OF FLESH

In the natural realm, man speaks through breath.

In the realm of glory, God speaks through Presence.

The psalmist said:

> *"The voice of the LORD is powerful;*
> *the voice of the LORD is full of majesty."*
> *— Psalm 29:4*

The word majesty is linked to glory.

When God speaks, glory vibrates.

when glory vibrates, the soul receives revelation.

No one hears God casually.

His voice flows out of:

- His holiness

- His weight

- His nature

- His presence

This is why only the pure in heart perceive His voice.

2. THE VOICE OF GOD IS A GLORY-VOICE, NOT A HUMAN WHISPER

God told Moses:

*"...there I will meet with you,
and I will speak with you from above the mercy seat..."*
— Exodus 25:22

This means:

**The voice of God does not come from earth upward —

it comes from heaven downward. **

It is a throne-voice.

It is judicial.

It is authoritative.

It is creative.

It is transformative.

His voice carries the same power that created the universe.

3. THE GLORY REALM IS THE REALM OF REVELATION

Paul reveals:

"...God... has shone in our hearts to give the light of the knowledge of His glory..."
— 2 Corinthians 4:6

Revelation is not information—

it is illumination.

It is the unveiling of things hidden.

It is the manifestation of God's mind.

The believer hears God clearly when:

- the heart is purified

- the spirit is yielded

- the mind is renewed

- the atmosphere is filled with glory

Glory is the environment in which revelation becomes natural.

4. THE VOICE OF GOD IS MULTI-DIMENSIONAL

Scripture reveals God speaks in many ways:

A. The Audible Voice

Moses on Sinai, Samuel in the Temple, Jesus at the Jordan.

B. The Still, Small Voice

Elijah in the cave (1 Kings 19:12).

The Hebrew here means a whisper of gentle silence.

C. The Inner Witness of the Spirit

Romans 8:16 — The Spirit bears witness.

D. Dreams and Visions

Joel 2:28, Acts 2:17.

E. Scripture Illuminated

The Word becomes fire, revelation, instruction.

F. Prophetic Utterance

The Holy Spirit speaking through a vessel.

G. Angelic Messages

Old and New Testament examples.

Each expression of God's voice is tied to His glory.

Where the glory is absent, revelation becomes faint.

Where the glory is present, revelation becomes clear.

5. GLORY MAKES THE HEART A PROPHETIC RECEIVER

Jesus said:

"...My sheep hear My voice..."
— John 10:27

Hearing is not optional in the kingdom —

it is identity.

When glory rests on a person:

- the heart becomes tender

- the spirit becomes receptive

- the ears become open

- the mind becomes illuminated

This is why the prophets were glory-carriers.

Glory sharpens prophetic perception.

6. THE GLORY REALM AND THE SPIRIT OF PROPHECY

Revelation 19:10 declares:

"...the testimony of Jesus is the spirit of prophecy."

Meaning:

In the glory, everything God says reveals Jesus.

Prophecy is not prediction —

it is revelation of Christ.

Prophecy flows from:

- an atmosphere of glory

- the mind of Christ

- the heart of the Father

- the utterance of the Spirit

This is why authentic prophecy requires consecration.

7. THE VOICE OF GOD CARRIES CREATIVE POWER

Psalm 29 continues:

- His voice breaks cedars

- His voice divides flames

- His voice shakes the wilderness

- His voice strips forests

- His voice thunders

These are glory effects.

When God speaks:

- demons flee

- sickness breaks

- atmospheres shift

- nature responds

- the human spirit awakens

- destiny ignites

The voice of God is glory in verbal form.

8. DISOBEDIENCE DIMINISHES HIS VOICE; OBEDIENCE AMPLIFIES IT

Jesus said:

> *"If anyone wills to do His will,*
> *he shall know…"*
> *—John 7:17*

Revelation increases with obedience.

Rebellion deafens the soul.

The more a believer obeys,

the clearer the voice of God becomes.

The less a believer obeys,

the more distant the voice becomes.

Obedience is spiritual hearing.

9. INTIMACY SHARPENS DISCERNMENT

Discernment is not suspicion.

It is not intuition.

It is not emotional reaction.

Discernment is:

- recognizing the Shepherd's voice

- distinguishing between holy and unholy

- sensing the movements of the Spirit

- detecting deception

- knowing the will of God

Discernment is conceived in intimacy

and matured in glory.

10. THE VOICE OF GOD BECOMES A LIFESTYLE IN THE GLORY REALM

For the mature believer:

- prayer becomes conversation

- revelation becomes continuous

- prophetic flow becomes natural

- guidance becomes intuitive

- Scripture becomes alive

The voice of God becomes not an event,

but the rhythm of life.

This is the highest state of spiritual maturity:

walking under the canopy of glory and listening as a son listens to a Father.

THE FINAL REVELATION OF THIS CHAPTER

The glory of God is not silent.

It speaks.

It instructs.

It reveals.

It illuminates.

It commands.

It comforts.

It corrects.

It directs.

Glory is the atmosphere of God's voice.

The voice is the expression of God's glory.

To dwell in glory is to dwell in revelation.

To walk in glory is to walk in divine communication.

And to hear God clearly is not a gift given to a few —

it is the inheritance of every child born into His presence.

Here is the truth:

**Glory leads to intimacy.

Intimacy leads to hearing.

Hearing leads to obedience.

Obedience leads to greater glory. **

It is a cycle without end —

a journey into the heart of God

CHAPTER FIFTEEN: THE GLORY AND THE KINGDOM: HOW GOD ESTABLISHES HIS RULE THROUGH HIS PRESENCE

The glory of God is not just a spiritual experience;

it is the visible expression of God's Kingdom.

Where glory rests, God rules.

Where glory increases, the Kingdom advances.

Where glory departs, human systems take over.

Jesus did not preach a religion.

He preached a Kingdom.

And the Kingdom is not abstract.

It is a realm.

A power.

A government.

A dominion.

And the glory is the atmosphere of that dominion.

1. THE FIRST REVELATION: THE KINGDOM AND GLORY ARE INSEPARABLE

Paul wrote:

"For the kingdom of God is not in word but in power."
— 1 Corinthians 4:20

Power (dunamis) is a manifestation of glory.

Jesus said:

"The kingdom of God has come near you..."
— Luke 10:9

How was it near?

Because the glory was present in Him.

The Kingdom is the authority of God.

The glory is the manifestation of that authority.

The Kingdom is invisible.

The glory makes it visible.

Thus:

Where the Kingdom advances, the glory reveals it.

2. THE GLORY REALM IS THE SEAT OF GOD'S GOVERNMENT

Isaiah saw the throne:

> *"...high and lifted up..."*
> *— Isaiah 6:1*

Revelation shows the throne surrounded by:

- lightnings

- thunders

- voices

- fire

- rainbow glory

The throne is:

- the source of God's rule

- the center of God's Kingdom

- the origin of power

And the atmosphere of the throne is glory.

This means:

When glory rests on a person, God's throne is

being expressed through that person.

They carry governmental authority.

3. JESUS — THE KING OF GLORY AND THE KING OF THE KINGDOM

Psalm 24 calls Him:

> *"...the King of glory..."*

The Gospels call Him:

> *"...the King of the Jews..."*
> *"...the King eternal..."*
> *"...the King of the Kingdom..."*

He is the King of glory

because the Kingdom is carried in glory.

Where Jesus is enthroned, His glory manifests.

Where His glory manifests, His Kingdom advances.

4. THE KINGDOM WITHIN AND THE GLORY WITHIN

Jesus said:

> *"The kingdom of God is within you."*
> *— Luke 17:21*

Paul said:

> *"...Christ in you, the hope of glory."*
> *— Colossians 1:27*

Meaning:

The Kingdom within you is carried by the glory within you.

The believer becomes:

- a carrier of the Kingdom

- a representative of the King

- a vessel of dominion

- a temple of glory

- a gateway through which heaven enters earth

God establishes His Kingdom not by force, but by glory.

5. THE GLORY ADVANCES THE KINGDOM THROUGH TRANSFORMATION OF THE BELIEVER

The Kingdom begins inside and expands outward.

The Spirit transforms the believer:

- mind

- emotions

- desires

- character

- identity

Then through them transforms environments:

- families

- communities

- workplaces

- cities

- nations

Glory changes people.

Changed people change systems.

Transformation is the mechanism of Kingdom expansion.

6. THE GLORY ADVANCES THE KINGDOM THROUGH SIGNS, WONDERS, AND POWER

Jesus said:

> *"...if I cast out demons by the Spirit of God,*
> *then the kingdom of God has come upon you."*
> *— Matthew 12:28*

Miracles are proof of the Kingdom.

Deliverance is evidence of the Kingdom.

Healing is demonstration of the Kingdom.

These are not entertainment —

they are manifestations of glory enforcing divine government.

Where glory appears, the rule of Satan is broken.

7. THE GLORY ADVANCES THE KINGDOM THROUGH THE WORD OF THE KING

Jesus preached:

- the Gospel of the Kingdom

- the commandments of the Kingdom

- the mysteries of the Kingdom

- the righteousness of the Kingdom

The Spirit reveals these truths in the glory realm.

When the believer speaks from glory:

- the Word carries authority

- demons submit

- hearts open

- revelation penetrates

- destinies awaken

The Word becomes a sword of glory.

8. THE GLORY ADVANCES THE KINGDOM THROUGH WORSHIP

Worship is not singing.

It is enthronement.

The psalmist wrote:

> *"God is enthroned in the praises of Israel."*
> *— Psalm 22:3*

Where worship rises,

God's throne is established.

Where the throne is established,

His Kingdom manifests.

Where the Kingdom manifests,

glory descends.

Worship brings heaven to earth.

9. THE GLORY ADVANCES THE KINGDOM THROUGH PRAYER

Prayer is governmental.

It is legislative.

It is judicial.

Jesus said:

> *"…whatever you bind… whatever you loose…"*
> *— Matthew 18:18*

This authority flows not from emotion,

but from glory.

In the glory realm, prayer becomes:

- decree

- judgment

- legislation

- spiritual enforcement

The Kingdom advances through praying in alignment with heaven's government.

10. THE GLORY ADVANCES THE KINGDOM THROUGH UNITY

Unity is not agreement —

it is alignment.

Jesus prayed:

> *"...that they may be one,*
> *that the world may know..."*
> *— John 17:22–23*

Unity is the platform of glory.

Glory is the evidence of the Kingdom.

Where believers are united,

the Kingdom becomes visible.

Where unity is broken,

the Kingdom becomes obstructed.

Unity multiplies glory.

Glory multiplies Kingdom expression.

11. THE GLORY WILL FILL THE EARTH AS THE FINAL KINGDOM

Habakkuk prophesied:

> *"...the earth will be filled with the knowledge*
> *of the glory of the Lord..."*
> *— Habakkuk 2:14*

This is the final Kingdom:

- not a political kingdom

- not a religious kingdom

- not an earthly kingdom

But a kingdom filled with:

- glory

- light

- holiness

- righteousness

The age to come is a glory age.

The New Jerusalem shines with glory.

The Lamb radiates glory.

The saints reflect glory.

The nations walk in glory.

There is no sun —

because glory IS the light.

THE FINAL REVELATION OF THIS CHAPTER

The glory is not an accessory of the Kingdom.

It is the atmosphere of the Kingdom.

The Kingdom is not a doctrine.

It is a realm of glory.

The believer is not a spectator.

They are a carrier of glory,

an ambassador of the Kingdom,

a vessel of divine dominion.

Here is the truth:

**Glory establishes the King in the heart.

Kingdom establishes the glory in the earth. **

The purpose of the glory is to reveal the King.

The purpose of the Kingdom is to reveal His glory.

This is the destiny of every believer.

CHAPTER SIXTEEN: THE GLORY AND THE END-TIME CHURCH: THE RISE OF THE GLORIOUS BRIDE OF CHRIST

The Bible does not end with a suffering Church

or a silent Church

or a hiding Church.

Revelation ends with a glorious Church:

> *"...having the glory of God..."*
> *— Revelation 21:11*

Paul prophesied the same:

"...a glorious Church,
not having spot or wrinkle..."
— Ephesians 5:27

The end-time Church is marked not merely by doctrine,

or gifts,

or miracles—

but by glory.

This chapter explores the prophetic identity, character, and mandate of the generation that will carry the fullness of God's glory in the last days.

1. THE END-TIME GLORY WILL SURPASS FORMER GLORY

Haggai prophesied:

"The glory of the latter house

shall be greater than the former..."
— Haggai 2:9

This was not only about Zerubbabel's temple.

It was a prophetic sign of the final generation.

The first glory was:

- localized

- limited

- shadow-based

- restricted

The final glory is:

- global

- unlimited

- substance-based

- unveiled

The end-time Church will carry greater glory than Moses, Solomon, Elijah, or David ever saw.

2. THE END-TIME CHURCH WILL BE A BRIDAL CHURCH

The last-days identity of the Church is not an army first—

but a Bride.

Revelation 19 :7

> *"...His Bride has made herself ready..."*

Bridal identity means:

- intimacy

- purity

- devotion

- union

- love

- partnership

The glory rests most heavily on the Church that knows who she is.

Brides carry glory because brides carry on their garments the fragrance of the Bridegroom.

3. THE END-TIME CHURCH WILL BE A HOLY CHURCH

Glory rests on purity.

The last-days Church will be marked by:

- holiness

- consecration

- separation

- righteousness

- purity in speech, thought, and action

Isaiah 4:5–6 prophesies:

> *"...overall, the glory there will be a covering..."*

The covering of glory only comes where holiness is restored.

The end-time Church will be a holy remnant,

not a compromised multitude.

4. THE END-TIME CHURCH WILL BE AN ANOINTED CHURCH

Joel 2 and Acts 2 reveal:

- an outpouring of Spirit

- prophecy

- dreams

- visions

- supernatural signs

These are glory manifestations.

The Spirit poured out produces:

- revelation

- power

- miracles

- prophetic clarity

- apostolic authority

The Bride will move in dimensions of glory the early Church only tasted.

5. THE END-TIME CHURCH WILL WALK IN MIRACLE GLORY

Jesus said:

> *"...greater works than these shall you do..."*
> *—John 14:12*

Why greater works?

Because glory will increase.

The Acts Church healed the sick.

The glory Church will heal nations.

The Acts Church cast out demons.

The glory Church will dismantle demonic structures.

The Acts Church preached in power.

The glory Church will preach in unprecedented fire.

The end-time Church will return to:

- apostolic signs

- prophetic demonstrations

- healing glory

- deliverance fire

- miracle atmosphere

But at greater intensity.

6. THE END-TIME CHURCH WILL BE A VICTORIOUS CHURCH

Jesus said:

"...the gates of hell shall NOT prevail..."
— Matthew 16:18

The final Church is not:

- defeated

- hiding

- powerless

It is:

- radiant

- triumphant

- overcoming

- filled with glory

Revelation 12:11 describes a victorious people who:

- overcome by the blood

- overcome by the word

- overcome by not loving their lives unto death

Glory produces courage.

Glory produces boldness.

Glory produces victory.

7. THE END-TIME CHURCH WILL BE A CHURCH OF DEEP INTIMACY

Revelation 3:20 reveals Jesus knocking at the door of His Church.

Why?

Because the final move is not external—

it is internal.

The Bride will walk in:

- deep fellowship

- continual communion

- unbroken worship

- sustained prayer

- revelation knowledge

- the secrets of His heart

This intimacy produces glory—

and glory produces intimacy.

8. THE END-TIME CHURCH WILL CARRY THE TESTIMONY OF JESUS

Revelation 19 :10

> *"...the testimony of Jesus is the Spirit of prophecy..."*

This means the Church will:

- reveal Christ

- preach Christ

- demonstrate Christ

- carry the nature of Christ

- walk in the authority of Christ

The glory inside the Church will be a revelation of the glorified Christ in the world.

9. THE END-TIME CHURCH WILL BE A PERSECUTED CHURCH

Before glory is revealed,

persecution intensifies.

Daniel, Revelation, Jesus, Paul, and Peter all warn:

- darkness will increase

- nations will rage

- persecution will rise

- the faithful will be tested

But persecution does not kill glory —

it intensifies it.

The persecuted Church becomes the glorified Church.

10. THE END-TIME CHURCH WILL BE A CHURCH OF GREAT HARVEST

Isaiah 60 prophesies:

> *"Arise, shine, for your light has come,*
> *and the glory of the Lord is risen upon you..."*

Then:

> *"...nations will come to your light..."*

The glory attracts the lost.

Glory draws nations.

Glory awakens hearts.

Glory produces repentance.

The final harvest will be glory-driven,

not strategy driven.

11. THE END-TIME CHURCH WILL BE THE GLORY-COVERED CHURCH OF REVELATION 21

Revelation ends with:

> *"...the city had no need of the sun...*
> *for the glory of God illuminated it..."*

This is the destiny of the Church:

- to shine

- to radiate

- to carry the Lamb's light

- to reflect divine nature

- to dwell eternally in glory

The end-time Church begins that shining now,

before entering eternity.

THE FINAL REVELATION OF THIS CHAPTER

The Church of the last days is not fearful—

it is fearless.

Not hidden—

but shining.

Not shrinking—

but rising.

Not weak—

but glorious.

Not defeated—

but triumphant.

The end-time Church is:

- the glorious Bride

- the holy remnant

- the anointed army

- the prophetic company

- the Kingdom carriers

- the reflection of Christ

- the vessel of glory

- the light of the world

This generation will see:

- greater glory

- greater harvest

- greater signs

- greater intimacy

- greater warfare

- greater revelation

Because the Bride is preparing for the return of the King of Glory.

CHAPTER SEVENTEEN: THE GLORY AND TRUE WORSHIP: THE ALTAR, THE POSTURE, AND THE SOUND THAT BRINGS GOD'S PRESENCE INTO HIS CHURCH

If there is one truth that the modern Church must recover, it is this:

Where worship is restored, glory returns.

Where worship is corrupted, glory departs. **

From Genesis to Revelation, glory always follows worship —

not ordinary worship, but true, holy, Spirit-offered, heart-consuming worship.

This chapter reveals the biblical patterns, heavenly blueprint, and spiritual laws of the kind of worship that brings the glory of God into His Church.

1. THE FIRST TRUTH: TRUE WORSHIP IS NOT A SONG — IT IS SURRENDER

Jesus declared:

"The hour is coming, and now is,
when the true worshipers will worship the Father in spirit and truth..."
— John 4:23

He did not say "true singers"

but true worshipers.

The Greek word for worship (proskyneō, προσκυνέω) means:

- to kiss toward

- to bow low

- to fall prostrate

- to surrender completely

- to give oneself fully to the One adored

True worship does not begin on a stage —

it begins on an altar.

2. TRUE WORSHIP ALWAYS BEGINS WITH AN ALTAR — NOT WITH MUSIC

Before there was a tabernacle,

before there was a Temple,

before there was a priesthood,

before there was a choir…

There was an altar.

The altar is where:

- blood is shed

- flesh dies

- will is surrendered

- holiness is restored

- God is honored

The first mention of worship in Scripture is Abraham on Mount Moriah (Genesis 22).

And he was not singing —

he was sacrificing.

Revelation:

Glory does not descend on talent — it descends on surrendered lives.

3. TRUE WORSHIP INVITES GOD'S GLORY BECAUSE IT ENTHRONES HIM

Psalm 22:3 reveals a mystery:

"God is enthroned in the praises of His people."

Worship is not entertainment —

it is enthronement.

The Hebrew word for "praises" (tehillah) refers to:

- prophetic singing

- spontaneous sound

- Spirit-inspired worship

- glory expressions

When true worship rises,

God establishes His throne in that atmosphere —

and where God is enthroned,

glory fills the house.

This is what happened in Solomon's Temple:

> *"...the house was filled with a cloud... so that the priests could not stand..."*
> *— 2 Chronicles 5:14*

Worship enthroned God.

Glory answered.

4. TRUE WORSHIP IS HOLY — NOT CASUAL

God told Moses:

> *"Take your sandals off...*
> *for the place where you stand is holy ground."*
> *— Exodus 3:5*

In the presence of glory,

worship is not casual, familiar, careless, or fleshly.

True worship:

- trembles

- reveres

- bows low

- honors holiness

- recognizes the weight of His presence

Isaiah saw the seraphim cry "Holy, holy, holy"

and the foundations shook.

Holiness is the sound that attracts glory.

5. TRUE WORSHIP IS SPIRIT-BORN — NOT FLESH-PRODUCED

Jesus said:

> *"...God is Spirit,*
> *and those who worship Him must worship in spirit and truth."*
> *— John 4:24*

Spirit worship is:

- birthed by the Spirit

- sustained by the Spirit

- empowered by the Spirit

- directed by the Spirit

Fleshly worship is:

- emotional hype

- performance

- entertainment

- talent-driven

- self-centered

Spirit worship carries glory because:

Only what the Spirit births can host the God who is Spirit.

6. TRUE WORSHIP INVOLVES THE WHOLE HEART, NOT PARTIAL DEVOTION

Jesus rebuked Israel:

> *"...these people honor Me with their lips,*
> *but their heart is far..."*
> *— Matthew 15:8*

Worship that brings glory must involve:

- the heart

- the mind

- the will

- the emotions

- the posture

- the voice

- the life

Worship is not a segment of service —

it is the entire posture of the believer.

7. TRUE WORSHIP IS SACRIFICIAL — IT COSTS

SOMETHING

David said:

> *"I will not offer to the LORD*
> *that which costs me nothing."*
> *— 2 Samuel 24:24*

Worship without cost carries no glory.

The cost may be:

- surrender

- repentance

- obedience

- time

- pride

- comfort

- self-will

- idols

- distractions

The greater the cost,

the greater the glory.

8. TRUE WORSHIP BREAKS THE ATMOSPHERE FOR GOD TO MOVE

When Jehoshaphat faced three armies,

God told him:

As they worshiped:

- atmospheres shifted

- enemies turned on each other

- confusion entered the enemy camp

- victory manifested

Worship opens the heavens

and disrupts the enemy.

Glory comes when the worship is pure.

9. TRUE WORSHIP REQUIRES UNITY — ONE SOUND, ONE HEART

Before glory filled Solomon's Temple, Scripture says:

"...the singers and musicians were as ONE..."
— 2 Chronicles 5:13

ONE heart

ONE sound

ONE focus

ONE Spirit

ONE voice

ONE purpose

Unity creates a landing space for glory.

Division kills worship.

Worship kills division.

10. TRUE WORSHIP CARRIES THE SOUND OF HEAVEN

Worship that brings glory is not earthly —

it is heavenly.

Heaven's worship is:

- spontaneous

- continual

- holy

- undefiled

- Spirit-filled

- glory-centered

Heaven is not quiet.

Heaven is a realm of unceasing worship.

When the Church aligns with heaven's sound,

glory descends.

11. TRUE WORSHIP IS INTIMACY EXPRESSED

True worship flows from relationship, not ritual.

It says:

- "I love You more than the world."

- "I desire Your presence above everything."

- "I surrender my will to Yours."

- "I choose You above all else."

God seeks worshipers because He seeks companions of His heart.

Worship is the language of intimacy.

Intimacy is the breeding ground of glory.

12. TRUE WORSHIP MAKES THE CHURCH A TEMPLE OF GLORY

Peter says:

> *"...you are a spiritual house..."*
> *— 1 Peter 2:5*

Paul says:

> *"...you are the temple of the Holy Spirit..."*
> *— 1 Corinthians 6:19*

When worship rises:

- the temple is activated

- the altar is ignited

- the Spirit is stirred

- the glory fills the house

A worshiping Church is a glory-filled Church.

A quiet Church is a powerless Church.

THE FINAL REVELATION OF THIS CHAPTER

True worship is not:

- music

- performance

- talent

- tradition

- emotion

- atmosphere

True worship is:

- surrender

- sacrifice

- holiness

- Spirit-led honor

- intimacy

- enthronement

- unity

- obedience

- fire

- purity

And where true worship rises,

glory descends.

A worshiping Church will always be a glorious Church.

A glorious Church will always be a victorious Church.

A victorious Church will always reveal Jesus to the world.

This is the worship God is restoring in the last days —

the worship that draws the King of Glory into His sanctuary.

CHAPTER EIGHTEEN: THE GLORY AND THE HOUSE OF PRAYER: THE ALTAR OF INTERCESSION THAT SUSTAINS GOD'S PRESENCE IN HIS CHURCH

Jesus declared with burning conviction:

"My house shall be called a HOUSE OF PRAYER..."
— Matthew 21:13

Not a house of music.

Not a house of programs.

Not a house of preaching.

Not a house of gatherings.

But a House of Prayer.

Why ?

Because prayer is the breathing of the Spirit,

the incense of heaven,

the altar of intercession,

and the primary atmosphere in which the glory of God rests.

This chapter reveals the theological, prophetic, priestly dynamics that connect the glory of God with a praying Church.

1. THE FIRST REVELATION: GLORY RESTS WHERE THERE IS PRAYER

Every major glory manifestation in Scripture is preceded by prayer:

- Moses on Sinai

- Elijah on Carmel

- David in the sanctuary

- Solomon dedicating the temple

- Isaiah in the temple

- Daniel seeking God with fasting

- Jesus praying before the Transfiguration

- The disciples praying in the upper room

- The early Church praying in one accord

Prayer builds the atmosphere.

Glory fills it.

Prayer invites glory.

Glory answers prayer. **

2. PRAYER IS INCENSE — THE FRAGRANCE THAT ATTRACTS GOD'S PRESENCE

In the tabernacle, the golden altar of incense stood before the veil, closest to the glory.

Revelation reveals :

> *"...the golden bowls full of incense,*
> *which are the prayers of the saints."*
> *— Revelation 5 :8*

Incense symbolizes:

- purity

- devotion

- worship

- intercession

- surrender

Where incense rises, glory descends.

Prayer is not ritual —

it is fragrance.

3. THE HOUSE OF PRAYER IS GOD'S CHOSEN DWELLING PLACE

God told Solomon:

"...My eyes and My heart will be there perpetually."
— *2 Chronicles 7:16*

Where?

The house of prayer.

A praying Church becomes:

- a resting place for His presence

- a throne room expression on earth

- a sanctuary of glory

- a place where His eyes watch

- a place where His heart dwells

Prayer houses God.

God houses glory.

Thus, prayer houses glory.

4. PRAYER IS THE LIFEBLOOD OF GLORY — WITHOUT IT, THE FIRE DIES

Leviticus 6:13:

"The fire shall ever be burning; it shall NEVER go out."

How was the fire sustained?

Through continual offerings — the priestly ministry of prayer.

The moment prayer stops:

- the altar cools

- the fire fades

- the presence lifts

- the glory withdraws

Prayer sustains glory because prayer sustains the altar.

The altar sustains the fire.

The fire sustains the glory.

5. THE GLORY AND INTERCESSION — PARTNERS IN THE SPIRIT

Intercession brings:

- breakthrough

- protection

- deliverance

- visitation

- revival

- healing

- transformation

Moses interceded and the glory returned to Israel.

Daniel interceded and glory broke Babylon's timing.

Anna interceded and glory birthed Messiah in the temple.

The apostles interceded and glory shook the room.

Intercession is the labor room of glory.

6. THE MOST POWERFUL PRAYERS ARE BIRTHED IN THE GLORY

Romans 8:26:

"…the Spirit Himself makes intercession through us…"

This is not human prayer —

it is Spirit-generated intercession.

In the glory realm:

- prayer becomes prophetic

- prayer becomes authoritative

- prayer becomes fire

- prayer becomes decree

- prayer becomes divine warfare

- prayer becomes kingdom enforcement

Glory-empowered prayer shakes nations.

7. A HOUSE OF PRAYER IS A HOUSE OF GLORY-GOVERNMENT

In prayer, the Church:

- binds and looses

- legislates in the spirit

- shifts atmospheres

- dethrones demonic powers

- establishes Kingdom rule

- releases angelic assignment

- enforces God's will

Prayer is governmental.

It is judicial.

It is legislative.

A praying Church becomes a governmental Church.

Where government is established, glory remains.

8. PRAYER AND WORSHIP — THE TWO WINGS OF GLORY

Worship ascends.

Prayer ascends.

Both create:

- atmosphere

- habitation

- sanctification

- heavenly alignment

Worship enthrones God.

Prayer invites God.

Together, they host God.

This is why the early Church "continued steadfastly in prayer"—

and "great grace was upon them all."

Prayer + Worship = Glory.

9. UNITY IN PRAYER CREATES A GLORY INVASION

Acts 2:

> *"...they were all in one accord...*
> *and suddenly..."*

Acts 4:

> *"...they lifted their voice with one accord...*
> *and the place was shaken..."*

Unity multiplies prayer power.

Prayer multiplies glory power.

A divided Church cannot host glory.

A united praying Church becomes a habitation of heaven.

10. A HOUSE OF PRAYER BECOMES A GATE OF GLORY

Jacob saw:

- an open heaven

- angels ascending and descending

- the presence of God

- the gate of heaven

What produced the encounter?

Jacob built an altar.

Jacob prayed.

When a Church becomes a House of Prayer:

- heaven opens

- angels ascend and descend

- revelation flows

- miracles break out

- God's presence becomes tangible

Prayer opens the gate.

Glory comes through the gate.

11. THE END-TIME CHURCH WILL BE A GLOBAL HOUSE OF PRAYER

Isaiah prophesied:

"...My house shall be a house of prayer for ALL NATIONS."
— Isaiah 56:7

In the last days:

- prayer movements will rise

- intercessors will awaken

- night-and-day prayer will increase

- global worship will intensify

- houses of prayer will appear everywhere

- glory will fill regions

- revival will spread internationally

The end-time Church will be a 24/7 sanctuary of prayer and glory.

12. WHEN PRAYER CEASES, GLORY DEPARTS —

WHEN PRAYER RETURNS, GLORY RETURNS

The pattern is undeniable:

- Israel prayed → glory returned

- Solomon prayed → glory filled the Temple

- Daniel prayed → glory revealed mysteries

- The early Church prayed → glory shook cities

- The persecuted Church prayed → glory strengthened them

- The last days Church prays → glory covers the earth

The decline of prayer is always followed by the decline of glory.

The rise of prayer is always followed by the rise of glory.

THE FINAL REVELATION OF THIS CHAPTER

The greatest expression of the Church is not:

- talent

- programs

- production

- strategy

- intellectual preaching

The greatest expression of the Church is:

a praying people hosting the glorious presence of God.

Where prayer rises, glory falls.

Where prayer is continual, glory becomes continual.

Where the house becomes a House of Prayer,

the house becomes a House of Glory.

A Church that prays is a Church God dwells in.

A Church that prays is a Church God speaks in.

A Church that prays is a Church God fights for.

A Church that prays is a Church the enemy fears.

A Church that prays is a Church that changes nations.

Prayer is the altar.

Glory is the fire.

The Church is the temple.

This is the blueprint God is restoring in the last days.

CHAPTER NINETEEN: THE GLORY AND THE WORD: THE SCRIPTURE THAT ESTABLISHES, PURIFIES, AND REVEALS GOD'S PRESENCE IN HIS CHURCH

The Church of glory must also be the Church of Scripture.

No matter what dimension of glory God reveals,

no matter what experiences believers encounter,

no matter what manifestations appear —

The Word of God is still the final authority, the immovable standard, the eternal foundation, and the governing voice of the glory realm.

This chapter reveals why the Word and the glory are inseparable—

why the Spirit cannot move apart from the Word,

and why every true move of glory restores honor for the Scriptures.

1. THE FIRST REVELATION: THE WORD IS GLORY IN WRITTEN FORM

John declares:

"The Word became flesh and dwelt among us,

and we BEHELD His GLORY..."
— John 1:14

To behold Christ is to behold glory.

To behold the Word is to behold Christ.

Therefore:

To behold the Word is to behold glory.

The Word is not information —

it is manifestation.

It carries the nature, essence, power, and presence of God Himself.

2. THE GLORY RESTS WHERE THE WORD IS HONORED

In Nehemiah 8, when Ezra read the Word:

- people wept

- hearts trembled

- conviction fell

- revelation opened

- worship arose

- a national revival began

Why ?

Because glory comes where Scripture is restored.

Where the Word is honored:

- holiness increases

- purity strengthens

- worship deepens

- prayer becomes authoritative

- deception is exposed

- the Spirit moves freely

The glory settles on the house that honors the Word.

3. THE WORD CLEANSES THE CHURCH TO CARRY THE GLORY

Jesus declared:

> *"You are clean because of the Word..."*
> *— John 15:3*

Psalm 119:9 adds:

> *"How shall a young man cleanse his way?*
> *By taking heed according to Your Word."*

Glory requires purity.

Purity requires the Word.

The Word:

- purifies motives

- corrects doctrine

- sanctifies the mind

- cleanses the heart

- exposes hidden darkness

- renews the spirit

Glory cannot rest on an unwashed Church.

The Word is the water of cleansing.

4. THE WORD REVEALS THE GOD OF GLORY

The Word is not simply instruction —

it is revelation of God Himself.

David cried:

> *"Open my eyes, that I may behold*
> *WONDROUS things out of Your law."*
> *— Psalm 119:18*

The Hebrew word for wondrous (palaʾ, אָלָפ) means:

- supernatural

- miraculous

- glorious

Meaning:

The Scriptures contain glory waiting to be unveiled.

The more the Word is opened,

the more the glory is revealed.

5. THE GLORY REALM MAKES THE WORD COME ALIVE

Two disciples on the road to Emmaus said:

> *"Did not our hearts burn within us…*
> *when He opened the Scriptures to us?"*
> *— Luke 24:32*

The burning is the glory.

The opening is the revelation.

When the glory rests:

- Scripture burns

- Scripture speaks

- Scripture illuminates

- Scripture pierces

- Scripture transforms

- Scripture becomes living fire

Without glory, the Word seems distant.

With glory, the Word becomes a consuming flame.

6. THE WORD IS THE SWORD OF GLORY IN SPIRITUAL WARFARE

Paul calls the Word:

> *"...the sword of the Spirit..."*
> — *Ephesians 6:17*

The sword is the Word.

But the sword only has power when the Spirit wields it.

Glory empowers the Word for warfare:

- to break chains

- to cut demonic strongholds

- to silence the enemy

- to expose lies

- to execute divine judgment

- to shift atmospheres

A Word-filled believer is a glory-filled warrior.

7. THE WORD PROTECTs THE CHURCH FROM COUNTERFEIT GLORY

Satan can imitate:

- manifestations

- emotions

- power

- supernatural signs

- spiritual experiences

But Satan cannot imitate Scripture truth.

A Church without the Word:

- is open to deception

- will follow false manifestations

- will be seduced by emotional worship

- may mistake strange fire for holy fire

- can be manipulated by false prophets

- becomes spiritually unstable

But a Church anchored in the Word:

- discerns truth

- tests spirits

- recognizes error

- guards holiness

- protects the glory

- remains unshakable

The Word is the fence that protects the glory.

8. THE WORD IS THE FOUNDATION OF TRUE WORSHIP

Jesus said:

> *"Sanctify them in truth;*
> *Your Word is truth."*
> *— John 17:17*

Worship must be grounded in truth, or it becomes idolatry.

Without the Word:

- worship becomes emotional entertainment

- doctrines drift

- lyrics become unscriptural

- feelings replace revelation

- glory departs

Worship must carry the weight of Scripture

for glory to rest on it.

9. THE WORD IS THE FUEL OF PRAYER AND INTERCESSION

The early Church prayed Scripture constantly.

When they prayed Psalm 2 in Acts 4:

- the place shook

- boldness came

- glory filled the room

Scripture-saturated prayer carries glory authority.

Praying the Word:

- aligns the believer with heaven

- increases spiritual accuracy

- sharpens prophetic expression

- drives out fear

- brings angelic activity

- enforces God's decrees

A praying Church without Scripture is powerless.

A praying Church with Scripture is unstoppable.

10. THE END-TIME GLORY MOVEMENT WILL RESTORE DEEP LOVE FOR THE WORD

Amos prophesied a famine of the Word (Amos 8:11).

But the end-time Church will reverse it.

In the last days, God will raise:

- Word-filled worshipers

- Word-rooted intercessors

- Word-centered preachers

- Word-grounded prophets

- Word-disciplined disciples

The last great glory movement will not be:

- shallow

- emotional

- entertainment-driven

- personality-driven

It will be Word-driven.

Because only the Word can sustain the weight of the glory God is releasing.

THE FINAL REVELATION OF THIS CHAPTER

The glory and the Word are inseparable.

The Word reveals the glory.

The glory illuminates the Word.

The Spirit breathes on both.

Where the Word is exalted,

glory descends.

Where the Word is obeyed,

glory remains.

Where the Word is lived,

glory increases.

Where the Word is preached,

glory transforms nations.

No glory movement can survive without the Word.

And no Word movement is complete without the glory.

The Word is the foundation.

The glory is the expression.

Together, they reveal Jesus Christ,

the living Word,

the King of Glory.

**FINAL PRAYER

A Cry for Glory, A Surrender to His Presence**

O Father of Glory,

God of light, majesty, and unsearchable beauty—

we bow before You with trembling hearts

and lifted hands,

acknowledging that You alone are worthy.

From everlasting to everlasting,

You have dwelt in unapproachable light.

You rode upon the wings of the wind.

You stretched out the heavens like a curtain.

You breathed galaxies into existence.

You formed man from the dust

and crowned him with glory.

And yet—

in Your unfathomable mercy—

You invite us to come near.

We bow before You,

asking not for blessings,

not for earthly gain,

not for temporary comfort,

but for Your glory.

Lord, let Your glory fill Your Church again

until every idol falls,

every heart burns,

every mind transforms,

every family is restored,

every chain is broken,

and every believer reflects the radiant image of Christ.

Father, restore to us

the awe that trembles,

the holiness that separates,

the worship that surrenders,

the prayer that prevails,

the faith that sees the invisible,

and the devotion that refuses to let go.

Consume us in Your fire.

Purify us with Your Word.

Sanctify us by Your Spirit.

Cover us with the blood of the Lamb.

Clothe us with humility.

Fill us with wisdom.

Lead us into deeper intimacy with You.

Make us a people of Your presence,

a dwelling place for Your glory,

a royal priesthood who tend the altar day and night

until Your will is done on earth

as it is in heaven.

O King of Glory—

step through the ancient gates of our hearts.

Take Your rightful place upon the throne of our lives.

Let Your Kingdom come,

and let Your glory be revealed.

And when our journey on this earth is complete,

when time gives way to eternity,

and when faith becomes sight—

bring us into Your eternal glory,

where we shall behold Your face,

walk in Your light,

and dwell in Your presence forever and ever.

Until that day,

keep us faithful,

keep us watchful,

keep us burning with holy fire,

and keep us standing firm

in the hope of Your returning.

We pray all this

in the matchless, majestic, glorious name

of Jesus Christ,

the King of Glory,

the Lamb upon the Throne,

and the Light of Eternity.

Amen and Amen.

**CLOSING REFLECTION

Standing at the Edge of Glory**

As you arrive at the final pages of this journey,

pause for a moment…

breathe deeply…

and let your heart become still.

You have walked through divine mysteries—

from the first revelation of glory,

to the fire of transformation,

to the intimacy of worship,

to the power of prayer,

to the authority of the Kingdom,

to the destiny of the Bride,

and finally,

to the eternal glory where God dwells forever.

Now the question remains…

What will you do with the glory you have encountered?

For glory is not merely a study—

it is an invitation.

It is not a doctrine—

it is a calling.

It is not a concept—

it is a realm of life.

And it is calling your name.

The glory of God longs to rest upon a willing heart,

a humble spirit,

a surrendered vessel.

The Lord waits for those who:

- desire Him above all things

- seek His face with undivided devotion

- embrace holiness without compromise

- choose intimacy over activity

- honor His Word

- cultivate a life of prayer

- worship from the altar of surrender

Not everyone will answer this call.

Not every believer will pay the price.

Not every church will host His presence.

Not every generation will walk in His fullness.

But those who do…

those who choose the narrow way…

those who say, "Here am I, Lord—take all of me" …

they will become carriers of His presence,

bearers of His light,

temples of His glory

in a world growing ever darker.

The glory of God is both invitation and responsibility.

It asks for your heart.

It asks for your obedience.

It asks for your surrender.

It asks for your life.

But in return…

it gives you Him.

His presence.

His love.

His power.

His beauty.

His voice.

His peace.

His Kingdom.

His eternal glory.

As you close this book,

know this one truth:

You were created for His glory.

Redeemed for His glory.

Shaped for His glory.

And destined to dwell in His glory forever. **

So, lift your eyes.

Set your heart on the eternal.

Consecrate your life once more.

And step boldly into the invitation of heaven:

"Arise, shine ;

for your light has come,

and the glory of the Lord

is risen upon you."
— Isaiah 60:1

The journey has not ended—

it has only begun.

www.ingramcontent.com/pod-product-compliance
Lightning Source LLC
Chambersburg PA
CBHW032233050726

47591CB00001B/378